Number 145
Spring 2015

New Directions for Evaluation

Paul R. Brandon
Editor-in-Chief

Accreditation, Certification, and Credentialing: Relevant Concerns for U.S. Evaluators

James W. Altschuld
Molly Engle
Editors

ACCREDITATION, CERTIFICATION, AND CREDENTIALING: RELEVANT CONCERNS FOR U.S. EVALUATORS
James W. Altschuld, Molly Engle (eds.)
New Directions for Evaluation, no. 145
Paul R. Brandon, Editor-in-Chief

Microfilm copies of issues and articles are available in 16mm and 35mm, as well as microfiche in 105mm, through University Microfilms Inc., 300 North Zeeb Road, Ann Arbor, MI 48106-1346.

New Directions for Evaluation is indexed in Academic Search Alumni Edition (EBSCO Publishing), Education Research Complete (EBSCO Publishing), Higher Education Abstracts (Claremont Graduate University), SCOPUS (Elsevier), Social Services Abstracts (ProQuest), Sociological Abstracts (ProQuest), Worldwide Political Science Abstracts (ProQuest).

NEW DIRECTIONS FOR EVALUATION (ISSN 1097-6736, electronic ISSN 1534-875X) is part of The Jossey-Bass Education Series and is published quarterly by Wiley Subscription Services, Inc., A Wiley Company, at Jossey-Bass, One Montgomery Street, Suite 1200, San Francisco, CA 94104-4594.

SUBSCRIPTIONS for individuals cost $89 for U.S./Canada/Mexico/international. For institutions, $358 U.S.; $398 Canada/Mexico; $432 international. Electronic only: $89 for individuals all regions; $358 for institutions all regions. Print and electronic: $98 for individuals in the U.S., Canada, and Mexico; $122 for individuals for the rest of the world; $430 for institutions in the U.S.; $470 for institutions in Canada and Mexico; $504 for institutions for the rest of the world.

All issues are proposed by guest editors. For proposal submission guidelines, go to http://www.eval.org/p/cm/ld/fid=48. Editorial correspondence should be addressed to the Editor-in-Chief, Paul R. Brandon, University of Hawai'i at Mānoa, 1776 University Avenue, Castle Memorial Hall Rm 118, Honolulu, HI 96822-2463.

www.josseybass.com

Cover photograph by ©iStock.com/Smithore

Editorial Policy and Procedures

New Directions for Evaluation, a quarterly sourcebook, is an official publication of the American Evaluation Association. The journal publishes works on all aspects of evaluation, with an emphasis on presenting timely and thoughtful reflections on leading-edge issues of evaluation theory, practice, methods, the profession, and the organizational, cultural, and societal context within which evaluation occurs. Each issue of the journal is devoted to a single topic, with contributions solicited, organized, reviewed, and edited by one or more guest editors.

The editor-in-chief is seeking proposals for journal issues from around the globe about topics new to the journal (although topics discussed in the past can be revisited). A diversity of perspectives and creative bridges between evaluation and other disciplines, as well as chapters reporting original empirical research on evaluation, are encouraged. A wide range of topics and substantive domains is appropriate for publication, including evaluative endeavors other than program evaluation; however, the proposed topic must be of interest to a broad evaluation audience.

Journal issues may take any of several forms. Typically they are presented as a series of related chapters, but they might also be presented as a debate; an account, with critique and commentary, of an exemplary evaluation; a feature-length article followed by brief critical commentaries; or perhaps another form proposed by guest editors.

Submitted proposals must follow the format found via the Association's website at http://www.eval.org/Publications/NDE.asp. Proposals are sent to members of the journal's Editorial Advisory Board and to relevant substantive experts for single-blind peer review. The process may result in acceptance, a recommendation to revise and resubmit, or rejection. The journal does not consider or publish unsolicited single manuscripts.

Before submitting proposals, all parties are asked to contact the editor-in-chief, who is committed to working constructively with potential guest editors to help them develop acceptable proposals. For additional information about the journal, see the "Statement of the Editor-in-Chief" in the Spring 2013 issue (No. 137).

Paul R. Brandon, Editor-in-Chief
University of Hawai'i at Mānoa
College of Education
1776 University Avenue
Castle Memorial Hall, Rm. 118
Honolulu, HI 968222463
e-mail: nde@eval.org

CONTENTS

EDITORS' NOTES

A s charter members of the American Evaluation Association (AEA) and being active in its predecessor organizations, we have an extensive history of discussing, reviewing, debating, and wondering about accreditation, certification, and credentialing (ACC). We are long-term collaborators (over 34 years) who have been involved continuously in presenting and writing about the preparation of evaluators and certification. In the early 1990s as an AEA board member, Engle recruited (cajoled, actually) Altschuld to lead a new directory of evaluation preparation programs.

This effort led to a *New Directions in Program Evaluation* (now *New Directions for Evaluation* [NDE]) issue (No. 62) published in 1994. We note this earlier result because it relates to the current issue. The first coeditor was communicating with the NDE Editor-in-Chief about an issue on needs assessment (Engle is a contributor to it). In that conversation, it was mentioned that she and I were recommended for an update to the 1994 publication focusing on the interconnected ideas of ACC.

Wow! What an opportunity to reconsider a topic that was done two decades ago, especially given the vastly changing context of the practice of evaluation, the theoretical understandings of it, and what has happened and is happening with professional organizations. We were delighted to be thought of for the task and the rest of the story is, as they say, "history."

This issue is not an update of the 1994 effort, nor is it intended to be: its focus is on interconnecting and dissecting ideas relative to ACC. We wanted to take a fresh look at them and we wanted our chapter authors to do the same thing. To that end, we assembled a diverse group of individuals with unique viewpoints to be our writers.

We debated how to start the current journey and felt that looking into ACC necessitated placing the three components in the historical context of how evaluation has evolved in the United States since the 1960s. We are not advocating for ACC; rather, we illuminate what their nature is and how past and current conditions have influenced thinking about them. We see the three parts of ACC as interrelated, and as critically important to any discussion of our field.

We start the discussion of the historical context by creating a timeline from the 1960s to the present (although we are sure that some events are omitted, making this a personal expression of history, not an actual one). This is the core content in Chapter 1 ("The Inexorable Historical Press of the Developing Evaluation Profession") written by us. In what ways do the past and the present inform and guide us relative to ACC? The

NEW DIRECTIONS FOR EVALUATION, no. 145, Spring 2015   © 2015 Wiley Periodicals, Inc., and the American Evaluation Association.   Published online in Wiley Online Library (wileyonlinelibrary.com) • DOI: 10.1002/ev.20107 chapter also contains definitions of terms and how changes in evaluation have affected ACC.

Having set the stage, we challenged our authors to go beyond simply providing an update of what is going on at present; we asked them to delve into the subtle and problematic concerns that are part of all the components of ACC. They were up to the responsibility, and we are grateful for their openness and willingness to accept this charge without flinching.

The focus of Chapter 2 ("Competencies for Program Evaluators in Light of Adaptive Action: What? So What? Now What?"), by Jean A. King and Laurie Stevahn, addresses the competencies that define evaluators. This is a tricky consideration, and an ACC issue without it would certainly miss the mark. These two authors, along with others, have been studying competencies (and competent practice) for nearly 15 years and are known throughout the world for their publications and in-depth research and thinking about this area. They have done an excellent job of dealing with concepts, examining salient research, and then raising questions that force evaluators to be more thoughtful in regard to specifying what they bring to the table via their services to programs and projects.

With this backdrop of competencies, it would seem a simple matter to describe the educational environment necessary for evaluators. Put simply, "Where do individuals acquire the skills and culture of the professional evaluator?" We knew the answer wasn't straightforward and sought out John M. LaVelle and Stewart I. Donaldson for preparing Chapter 3 ("The State of Preparing Evaluators"). In the past few years they have been conducting research about the nature of programs at universities and just recently completed another study. But like everything else in the field, preparation is now extensively offered in many venues other than academia. What does the educational picture look like and what might it become in the near future? The landscape they draw for us opens vistas to a quite complex scene.

What role does or should accreditation play in the ACC scenario was the question posed to James C. McDavid and Irene Huse for Chapter 4 ("How Does Accreditation Fit Into the Picture?"). McDavid and Huse are Canadians who authored a major text on evaluation and who were instrumental in writing the 2006 literature review that was the underpinning of the 2009 Canadian Evaluation Society's Credentialed Evaluator Designation system for program evaluators. With expanding educational and employment options, the field must be concerned with accreditation of evaluator preparation programs. How should evaluation as a budding profession go about ensuring their validity and quality? This consideration was raised by AEA in the 1990s and is as meaningful now as it was then. McDavid and Huse's vast knowledge of the field gets us closer to a response.

As briefly mentioned above, Canada initiated a system that is becoming known to many evaluators in the United States and in the world. It could

NEW DIRECTIONS FOR EVALUATION • DOI: 10.1002/ev

be a standard or benchmark from which U.S. evaluators could benefit and grow. Keiko Kuji-Shikatani, who has been active in the implementation of that system, graciously agreed to describe where things are at the present time, as well as what has been learned about dos and don'ts. This is the substance of Chapter 5 ("Credentialed Evaluator Designation Program, the Canadian Experience"). This chapter should be looked at in terms of what might or might not be applicable to U.S. evaluators and to our national organization (AEA). Put in a nutshell, "Does it make sense for us?"

"Evaluator Certification and Credentialing Revisited: A Survey of American Evaluation Association Members in the United States" is the title of Chapter 6 by Michelle Baron Seidling. The coeditors of this issue and several of the chapter authors were part of an AEA panel organized by Seidling for the 2012 annual meeting. From that discussion evolved a current national survey on certification (to be compared to the one done by Jones and Worthen [1999]). Results of the new survey were mixed without a clear mandate for either certifying or credentialing. What are the members' views? What do they think about ACC? Has opinion changed since the original work was done and, if so, in what ways? What guidance could/would this provide to AEA? The results are interesting and provocative.

Chapter 7, "Accreditation, Certification, and Credentialing: Does It Help?," represents a difficult undertaking. We wanted an independent voice to look at the overall proposition of accreditation, credentialing, and certification. Arguments can readily be raised about moving forward or doing nothing at all. Thinking about ACC, the profession has survived, even thrived, by doing nothing. An independent thinker was needed to critically analyze what the chapter authors have explained and to give some thoughtful conclusions about what they have provided. We chose Gene Shackman based on his reputation for following his own drummer. He has clearly done so and it is appreciated.

It was and remains our goal to encourage and expand the discussion on ACC but not to advocate for or against any of the three. If this issue of *New Directions* expands discourse and deliberation, then we have achieved what we intended personally and professionally. Please join us in the journey.

Reference

Jones, S. C., & Worthen, B. R. (1999). AEA members' opinions concerning evaluator certification. *American Journal of Evaluation, 20*, 495–506.

James W. Altschuld
Molly Engle
Editors

NEW DIRECTIONS FOR EVALUATION • DOI: 10.1002/ev

JAMES W. ALTSCHULD is professor emeritus at the College of Education and Human Ecology, The Ohio State University.

MOLLY ENGLE is a professor at the College of Education and evaluation specialist at Oregon State University Extension Service.

NEW DIRECTIONS FOR EVALUATION • DOI: 10.1002/ev

Altschuld, J. W., & Engle, M. (2015). The inexorable historical press of the developing evaluation profession. In J. W. Altschuld & M. Engle (Eds.), *Accreditation, certification, and credentialing: Relevant concerns for U.S. evaluators. New Directions for Evaluation, 145,* 5–19.

1

The Inexorable Historical Press of the Developing Evaluation Profession

James W. Altschuld, Molly Engle

Abstract

The history of the field of evaluation is described over the past half century to set the context for examining accreditation, certification, and credentialing that are the foci of this New Directions for Evaluation *issue. What have been and are the current forces that guide us in regard to thinking about the three concepts? Understanding how evaluation is evolving is crucial for considering actions that might or might not be taken. To the extent possible this is done from a neutral stance without advocating or endorsing what should or could be done next.* © Wiley Periodicals, Inc., and the American Evaluation Association.

C hange is constant—an inevitable occurrence for individuals, organizations, and societies. It can be slow, gradual, and not noticeable. But if you came back to what you thought was the same place after 5 or 10 years, some features would be recognizable and others totally new. By the same token, it can be cataclysmic and metamorphic like a tornado. We want to talk about change, as it relates to evaluator certification and credentialing and preparation program accreditation. The overall topic is fraught with issues.

We are veterans at evaluation for more years than should be mentioned, with more than 80 cumulative years between us as well as being members of the American Evaluation Association (AEA), and the organizations from which it evolved. Age and experience made us witness to and participants in the small and large things that have occurred and how they link to evaluator accreditation, credentialing, and certification (ACC). Our involvement began in the early 1990s via publications, studies, and presentations. It started when Engle, as an AEA Board member, suggested and essentially recruited Altschuld to conduct and update the directory of evaluation preparation programs (Altschuld, Engle, Cullen, Kim, & Macce, 1994) and the discussion of the pedagogy of evaluation. Two decades have passed and we have continued as active players in the discussion.

Before going further, it is important to make distinctions among terms, lest there is confusion (Altschuld, 2005). *Accreditation* is the formal review of a preparation or educational program to see that it meets standards of a profession or discipline. The reviews are rigorous self-studies conducted at periodic intervals. *Certification* attests to a person's competence on specific skills and knowledge often determined by a test given right after preparation. Being certified is generally a one-time event, but in some cases re-certification may be required at a later time (every three or five years, for example). Certification may result in a license to practice that profession. Many (most) professions that have recertification require continuing professional education to maintain that certification.

Credentialing specifies that a person has the requisite knowledge, skills, and practical experiences to be deemed worthy of a credential or designation of such status. Most commonly, this is through a review by other professionals of a portfolio submitted by the individual who desires the credential for their work. *Licensure* is the right to practice in a field as conferred through a governing body or under the aegis of the government. It is a legal right to conduct work in a field and to receive compensation for it. There is a sharp demarcation between licensure and certification/credentialing that is demonstrated by an example.

One can be certified to be a doctor by virtue of having passed the medical boards, but not be licensed to practice medicine. If convicted of a crime or guilty of serious malpractice, you might have the appropriate certification and passed all the exams, but the state retains the right to license and may deny or revoke your license because of not adhering to guidelines for conduct. You will then be denied by law from performing the duties in question. If you persist, there are sanctions, penalties, and in the extreme even imprisonment. Every year in professions we see removal of licensure and subsequent inability to practice.

These distinctions often become blurred when professional groups engage in discussions about accreditation, certification, and credentialing. The three entities are related but it is important to keep in mind their overlapping and unique aspects when reviewing commentary about them. Please do so as you read this chapter on relevant evaluation history and the others in this issue of *New Directions for Evaluation*.

NEW DIRECTIONS FOR EVALUATION • DOI: 10.1002/ev

Relevant History

We present a summarized timeline (not all-inclusive) of what has taken place; what seems important relative to the three topics of credentialing, certification, and accreditation; what has had bearing on where the profession is now; and where it might be going in the future (Table 1.1)? The timeline is from the 1960s to 2014. We will then examine much of what has transpired. The historical lenses afford a perspective, and through them we are informing, not advocating for, what AEA and evaluators could do. That decision is for others to decide.

First, a caveat is necessary before we discuss the table. We are not historians and do not provide a full and exhaustive history. Instead, we offer a version as known to us, based on long tenure with AEA and predecessor organizations and participation in a number of key moments in the timeline. It is tempered by both formal and informal work we did for AEA. (This work includes Board decisions to form committees exploring these topics in the mid-1990s and early 2000s, formally identifying evaluation preparation programs in two commissioned studies, debating the issues at AEA, and being involved in many panels and other sessions over approximately 15 years.) Since a case is not being made for comprehensiveness, we apologize if any authors or activities have not been noted. Conversely, enough information is provided to enable readers to develop reasoned opinions against the historical backdrop.

Note that a systems-type of concept is invoked here. One event has an impact on another, and they must be seen as interactive; as one event occurs, it collides with others, and their interactions and interplays produce a cumulative effect more than they would individually. Consequently, the suggestion is: Don't hone in on any one thing that has taken place when considering issues, but rather step back and think about the overall impact of the many. This is more difficult to do but is appropriate and leads to greater insights into the chapters in this issue of *New Directions for Evaluation*.

How the Past Informs Us—Emergent Themes

There is a lot of information in the table. Focusing on singular events in it loses much when compared to considering the overall nature of the history of evaluation. Consequently, we have extracted recurring and major themes as follows:

1. Evolution in ideas of evaluation as a field with more sophisticated practice.
2. An expanded body of literature.
3. Single professional society with affiliated local associations.

Table 1.1. Timeline of Some Trends/Directions Shaping Modern Evaluation as Related to Accreditation, Certification, and Credentialing

Time Period	Some Trends/Directions	Contributors/Comments
Mid-1960s–1970 The early years	Elementary and Secondary Education Act (ESEA) of 1965 called for the determination of needs for programs and projects Evaluation models/theoretical papers setting the basis for a profession Qualitative/quantitative dimensions of evaluation debated	Congress of the United States See early works by Stufflebeam (1973), Scriven (1973), Stake (1973), Alkin (1973), and others Nascent ideas of what evaluation is, the field of evaluation is being tilled
1970s The formative period	Evaluation textbooks appear Evaluation preparation programs are established Major evaluations are done Needs assessments as one area of evaluation are more noticeable Evaluation Network (ENET) and the Evaluation Research Society (ERS), predecessors of AEA, hold meetings Ohio Program Evaluators' Group formed Evaluation Kit is published (Altschuld at his first OPEG and ENET meetings in 1979; perhaps 200 were at the latter) Seeds of the qualitative and quantitative paradigm wars sown	Worthen and Sanders's (1973) text stands out First directory of evaluation preparation programs Evaluation of Sesame Street is produced Witkin's (1984) national study of educational needs assessments *Evaluation and Program Planning, Evaluation Review, and Educational Evaluation and Policy Analysis* begin to rise to prominence *Evaluation News* first published (to later become the *American Journal of Evaluation*) Prominent writers such as Guba (1978), Stufflebeam (1973), Scriven (1973), and others Worthen writes about evaluation as a profession
1980s through the early 1990s Teenage years toward maturity	Writings and books about evaluation ENET and ERS hold combined meetings (1981), eventually merge into AEA (1986) Topical Interest Groups (TIGs) more noticeable at AEA and obtain more status later	Publications and books increasing, such as Patton (1980, 1982) Paradigm wars ongoing; they set the foundation for mixed-methods practice, seen as a positive shift in how evaluations are carried out

(Continued)

Table 1.1. Continued

Time Period	Some Trends/Directions	Contributors/Comments
	Second evaluation preparation directory	Most evaluators now endorse mixed-methods practice
	Paradigm wars	Evaluation preparation in universities
	Local affiliates more numerous	AEA meetings growing in prestige, program, and number of attendees
	(1981: Engle meets Altschuld at the *Evaluation '81* meeting; they become long-term collaborators and friends)	
Early 1990s to the early 2000s	AEA fully emergent and the growth is being maintained	Plethora of authors and sources now on the scene (too many to single out)
Productive years moving toward adulthood	Third evaluation preparation directory published in 1994	Groundwork established for a virtual explosion in AEA membership
	TIGs become key players in the AEA annual program and a wide diversity of interests is apparent in them	AEA meetings attendance increases
	International attendees also present at annual AEA meetings	TIGs assume the role of key players in the meeting program
	From the middle to the end of the decade, the AEA Board commissions studies on certification and accreditation	Evaluator preparation programs studied in 1992–1994 showed a decline in number, perhaps due to the definition for what a program entails
	Articles on topics like those above were in a 1999 issue of the *American Journal of Evaluation*	The 1994 Directory in *New Directions for Program Evaluation* (Altschuld & Engle) and the issue also have content on evaluation as a profession, evaluator preparation, etc.
	Another article in the 1999 issue indicated that AEA membership was divided on the need for certification	Some AEA Board commissioned reports of certification and accreditation draw heavily on the writings of Canadians (see next entry)
	Evaluation topics shift, paradigm wars wane, and needs assessments move toward a hybrid framework of needs and assets	
	AEA professionally managed as demanded by growth	
	Logic-type maps more in evidence	

(Continued)

Table 1.1. Continued

Time Period	Some Trends/Directions	Contributors/Comments
Early 2000s through the end of the first decade Blossoming into full-fledged adulthood	AEA growth and change is a constant theme International presence at meetings maintained Many professional development (preparation) opportunities at the annual meeting A study of formal preparation programs suggests more programs are available than previously; may signal discipline growth Evaluator's Institute becomes a major force for preparation; some distance education programs AEA membership composition shifts from university base to a practitioner-focused one AEA Board moves to policy-oriented structure with day-to-day work assigned to the management group AEA electronic newsletter with topics devoted to technology; legislative efforts, and so forth Studies of skill sets usher in new looks about who evaluators are and what they do In 2009, the Canadian Evaluation Society votes for a credentialing system for evaluators; system launched shortly thereafter	AEA meetings have many attendees (see "Formative Period" when 200 were there in 1979) and sessions Meetings require major venues Changing composition of the group is notable More preparation options become available More programs may be there or possibly an artifact due to differences in definitions for what a program entails Stevahn, King, Ghere, and Minnema (2005), McGuire and Zorzi (2005), and others begin to study and document the skills of an evaluator McDavid and Huse (2006) develop a literature review about procedures for credentialing or certifying evaluators With the initiation of the new Canadian system, issues about accreditation, certification, and credentialing rise anew Association taking a proactive stance in regard to legislation and how evaluation might/should relate to it
The present and beyond Moving to and thinking about the future	New management firm chosen to handle AEA affairs Annual meeting attendance soars to over 3,000 Increasing diversity in members is apparent, and the TIGs fully cover a wide variety of interests More than 1,000 individuals take part in professional development programs	Pace of change could be accelerating Larger and larger meetings have effects (positive and negative) on AEA tenor The array of available ways for evaluators to be trained is more extensive than even in the late 1990s Many ideas to ponder as to what we want AEA to be and why we have those ideas

Note: The format of this table was based on one dealing with the history of needs assessment—see Altschuld and Watkins (in press).

4. Growth in the professional society into many areas and disciplines resulting in a shift out of education and educational psychology (they are still there but not as prominent) and in a much larger organization with an international presence.
5. Diversification in the nature of members' practice.
6. Changing (changed) preparation options.
7. Canada's credentialing process.

These are the salient themes emerging from the chronology in Table 1.1. Each will be looked at in light of their relationship to ACC. This hasn't been done previously, so we are estimating the effects. Other interpretations could be given and are to be expected. The intent is to provoke deliberation.

The text here is filtered through Worthen's (1994) discussion of a profession and how evaluation fares against criteria such as a specialized body of literature, a job market for skills, unique content, preparation programs, professional associations, standards for practice, and others. (Some additional sources to consider would be Altschuld [2005], Lysaght & Altschuld [2000], and McDavid & Huse [2006].)

Table 1.2 is a summary of the themes. For each entry in the first column, implications and commentary are provided.

How the Past Informs Us—Discussion

Let us look more closely at the themes. What are the deeper meanings in them especially as we begin to think about ACC and related actions that might be taken?

Evolution in Ideas of Evaluation as a Field With More Sophisticated Practice

As is evident from the tables, evaluation has evolved in a most emphatic manner. No longer is it an offshoot of another association such as Division H of the American Educational Research Association with its large number of evaluation-oriented members. Evaluation has gained ground and established its own turf as a full-fledged profession, or very close to one. A number of the criteria for being a profession, as described by Worthen, have been achieved. This is worlds apart from where the field was in the early 1970s.

One of the criteria not brought up previously was that at a certain developmental stage of a field, action typically is taken to deny entry of those who do not have the requisite skills and understandings deemed acceptable for membership. This may be when a person graduates from an accredited program of appropriate study and is signified as having attained the standards of the profession by certification (frequently by passing a competency test) or by being given a formal title or designation as per the Canadian

Table 1.2. Emergent Historical Themes and Implications for Accreditation, Certification, and Credentialing

Theme	Implications	Commentary
Evolution in ideas of evaluation as a field with more sophisticated practice	Broader, deeper understandings of evaluation would affect considerations of ACC Aside from literature-suggested basic skills, there is the issue of what content (models, procedures, specialized areas) should be in an evaluator's tool kit	Enriches, yet at the same time forces an intensive look at ACC Questions arise as to what should be the focus and content of ACC
Expanded body of literature	Rigor established through research and reporting	Establishes the continuing need for and expectations of research
Single professional society with affiliated local associations	One professional body to facilitate deliberations about ACC Many evaluators will look to AEA for guidance related to ACC Potentially many groups involved requiring a multitude of opinions and perceptions for decisions about the future	Local affiliates set own parameters; differ from national organization in regard to skills and backgrounds of their members Could ACC mandates impact (positively, negatively) the number of national/local members?
Growth in professional society	Growth in size could lead to possibly more bureaucratic structure for ACC; size affects potential changes. Some areas of evaluation such as preparation may have emphases on needs assessment, return on investment, and specific evaluation models, whereas others may not; how is this to be factored in? What should evaluation preparation consist of; questions of relative balance of skills, theory, history, and practical experience? With a notable international attendance and membership, how should that enter into discussions and possibilities?	Should there be a general approach to the three areas as well as additional specialized ones? What is the spread of models and approaches to be included in evaluator preparation? International programs for educational evaluators may be oriented to accountability systems; how would ACC deal with such situations?

(Continued)

Table 1.2. Continued

Theme	Implications	Commentary
Diversification in the nature of members' practice	As the membership has gone from primarily an academic base to a practitioner one in centers, consulting firms, and agencies, the effects may be large and dramatic What is the role of research in evaluation in relation to accrediting evaluator preparation programs; should it have a role?	If one were to certify by testing, what would be the relative weights of theory versus practice (i.e., certification for what)? In the ultimate sense, could such divisions exacerbate evaluator differences?
Changing (changed) preparation options	Might university programs with finite resource limitations give ground to other options such as The Evaluators Institute (TEI), distance programs, massive open online courses, etc.? Could a person receive designation through such preparation and experience even if they do not have an undergraduate or graduate degree? • How would this be done? • How would or should be compared to other pathways? • Has this possibility even been thought about? What about the maintenance of skills and content knowledge? How does continuing education affect this process?	The shift in preparation has been noteworthy What should preparation consist of, and can it ONLY be accomplished through traditional higher education mechanisms? What is required for evaluators to keep current, and how should this be done in terms of ACC Is this an individual or professional group responsibility?
Canada's credentialing process	What Canada has put in place makes it mandatory for AEA to look at the entire issue Evaluation is part of an international scene; what is going on elsewhere has bearing on what the United States thinks about and eventually does Canada created and initiated a model that the United States should carefully examine, even if we do nothing, something similar, or follow a different course	Could lead to a scenario where a designated Canadian evaluator markets his/her skills to a U.S. client and highlights having the status Behooves us to review what Canada initiated AEA must not be a silo

vernacular. Analogously, the first author of this chapter received a designation from the American Chemical Society upon completing a bachelor's degree in chemistry from an accredited program and the second author was certified to take the licensing exam offered by the Arizona State Board of Nursing because of her commencement from an accredited nursing program.

What Worthen (1994) noted as lacking in U.S. evaluation is still apparent; or is it? Perhaps relooking at the criteria he specified is valuable given the passage of time. Is evaluation a profession or not? If we assume that evaluation is, does it make sense for evaluators to incur the cost of accreditation, certification, or credentialing?

On the other hand, the evaluation field has prospered without establishing ACC. What is the outcome of pursuing these activities? People are trained and practice differently from one context to another; that has seemed to work well for going on 50 years. Is change necessary or even needed? Will implementing ACC really have a significant effect on practice? A practitioner in business-oriented preparation may gravitate toward Kirkpatrick's (1954) evaluation model for direction, and someone investigating a program or a project in another setting may see more merit in the Stufflebeam's CIPP model. The degree of fit may be more appropriate for one situation than another. These are illustrations of what has to be taken into consideration in AEA with its diverse membership.

Expanded Body of Literature

The explosion of venues available for the dissemination of evaluation findings is vast. When we first started in the field, there were few resources available to the evaluator. Currently, there are multiple journals and monographs, shelves of print resources, and perhaps even more resources online. Enter "evaluation" into a search engine and over 100,000,000 results are returned. That would tell you evaluation has had an effect.

Single Large Professional Society With Affiliated Local Associations

A large national organization with a notable number of local affiliates has emerged. Many different voices must come into deliberations about what the national organization is or should be, and that will affect all its parts. Local groups may have members who are more part-time in practice; their preparation and backgrounds could be somewhat disparate from those who look to the national level for a professional home. The U.S. professional society is much larger than the Canadian association; this may complicate ACC deliberations here. If actions are to be taken, like in any other system, they will have reverberations throughout.

Adequate time must be allowed for everyone to examine the pros and cons of what might be done. Input has to come from and be carefully thought about in relation to all parts of the AEA community. This must be

NEW DIRECTIONS FOR EVALUATION • DOI: 10.1002/ev

done systematically with conclusions reflecting multiple viewpoints. Collecting such information is no small matter as is incorporating many perspectives into decisions that are eventually made.

Growth in That Professional Society

The first three rows in Table 1.2 are subtle hues of the same fabric. They represent how much AEA has changed since this topic was first visited in the literature. One aspect of that change is the internationalization of the field as reflected in AEA membership. AEA has morphed from being solely a U.S. group to a more multicultural and multicountry society. The Board has included international representatives.

Contemplating ACC, how do they play against an international tapestry? The *Canadian Journal of Program Evaluation* recently published a special issue (King & Podems, 2014) that included reports on competencies (a basic consideration in ACC) from New Zealand, South Africa, and Russia, as well as Canada. Other countries have their own associations and forms of preparation and specialization in evaluation. How might anything that we do stack up with what is already available or done elsewhere? Some U.S.-based AEA members conduct evaluations in other countries and/or work heavily in developing ones. How should such ventures factor into ACC deliberations? Does getting certified or credentialed fully translate to conducting assessments of economic programs in sub-Saharan Africa or in impoverished areas of the Balkans or the Mideast? Would it relate to the cultural differences encountered in Indonesia or in situations of very top–down government control? Would it be meaningful to education where a ministry might mandate tight adherence to a national curriculum and ways to teach?

Adding to this, if AEA members were surveyed, some may or may not favor moving ahead on any of the topics associated with ACC. It might be imperative that survey results be disaggregated by domestic versus international foci to see if different perspectives affect the interpretation of results. The question is, What concerns are of importance to which segments of AEA members?

Diversification in Members and Changed Preparation Options

This refers to the fifth and sixth rows in Table 1.2. Using an example will demonstrate the impact of diversification. For years the first author has been presenting workshops and professional development sessions on needs assessment and associated methods. In 2013, he and Engle offered a workshop on conducting joint asset/capacity building and needs assessment projects. His tendency is to stress heavily the rationale behind those evaluation activities, bringing in research and theory. Engle, on the other hand, pushed for more hands-on activities. Admittedly, she was more on target. The AEA guidelines for professional development are very much in tune with her evaluation position not so much mine.

The field seems to want—no, demand—more a practice focus than a theoretical or research one. That isn't to imply that these are, or should be, in opposition, just that there is a difference and that the various mindsets need to be acknowledged. If the evaluator conducts evaluations as a practitioner, it may be of lesser import to want to know details of why something is to be done. Is the "why" less in comparison to the nature of procedures and how those procedures are implemented? We have seen hands-on approaches assume precedence. As time progresses, this distinction may become of greater importance.

Embedded in many parts of the tables are advance organizers and cues as to how diversification of practice and preparation options may affect ACC. Theory and courses on evaluation research may be more commonplace in university programs than in other forms of preparation. Professors are expected to publish, to push the knowledge boundary; practitioners not so much. Is it axiomatic that the history, the theoretical basis, and the research dimensions of evaluation would be stressed? The academy encourages students to do research leading to the submission of manuscripts and ultimate acceptance of the outcomes of that research. Although professors do implement projects, their livelihood is only partially determined by conducting evaluations.

Contrast this with an evaluation consultant where papers submitted for publication, while of value, are not as critical as writing proposals and seeking sources of financial support. Contracts have short-term permanence when looked at from a virtually guaranteed university-funded tenure line. The academic evaluator will not have the same tension or different ones than the practitioner who depends on his or her next grant.

How might these two aspects of evaluation (diversity of practice and preparation options) manifest in an ACC scenario? What should be an appropriate balance between theory, history, appreciation, and involvement in the evaluation literature when viewed through the ACC filter? What would be the effect of having different forms of accreditation for highly varied preparation options? If a practitioner-oriented shift in membership continues, we certainly gain some things, but there could be losses. The same argument could be directed to university programs. If a preparation program provides a certificate for participation, what does that certificate convey? To what skills or understandings does it attest?

Reversing the logic, we could ask the same thing about university preparation programs. What do the master's or doctoral degrees connote? In both examples, the underlying concern is the same: What do we expect an evaluator to know, understand, be able to do, and at what level of competency? We have lists of skills that have been systematically studied and verified. They are massive, and it is doubtful that any one person would have them all and be able to perform them at a consistently high level. One view might be that these are skill areas required for a team to do an evaluation, rather than a single individual. Many evaluations are done by collectives not individually. How are such judgments made especially in regard to certification or credentialing purposes?

Questions like those above have a uniquely positive dimension to them in that they force us to explore the composition of evaluators and what skills and knowledge should be included in their backgrounds. What methodology courses should they have taken and what are fundamental things for them to know. Aside from methodology, what about specialized evaluation content that should be included such as needs assessment, cost–benefit analysis, a variety of instrument construction techniques, use of surveys, how to plan and implement an evaluation, knowledge of the AEA evaluation standards and guiding principles, and ways of communicating evaluation findings to multifaceted audiences, among others? What content would constitute the minimum requirements or advanced preparation?

Canada's Credentialing Process

The last entry (Table 1.2) is the Canadian designation system for evaluators. This is a substantial endeavor done on a countrywide basis. It has been in existence for about four years and was in development for nearly three years prior to implementation. Its learning curve is worthy of study. What has worked and what hasn't? Has it had an effect on the practice of evaluation for better or worse? What costs have been incurred in start-up and what might be the continuing costs over time? What might have to be done for long-term maintenance in regard to personnel, upgrading, and other related matters? What insights and thoughts do its developers and implementers have? Has it led to more thought as to what preparation for evaluators should contain? What are issues regarding upgrading skills and learning new or different ones? Does it incorporate the concept of accreditation and, if so, in what ways? Could a designation affect current curriculums, might they be narrowed in accord with standards for the credentialing or might they become more diversified?

We see the Canadian work as a live experiment that provides much insight about credentialing. There will be carryover to accreditation and certification. We should appreciate the efforts of Canadian colleagues and be grateful for how they can inform our discussion.

Closing Note

The three related topics, accreditation, credentialing, and certification, are complex with many subtleties embedded in them. The intent of this chapter was not to offer a comprehensive look into their nature just enough detail to illuminate and expand thinking about them. We are confident that the authors of the other chapters will add much more meat to what is really a basic scaffold in this one.

NEW DIRECTIONS FOR EVALUATION • DOI: 10.1002/ev

References

Alkin, M. (1973). Excerpts from evaluation theory and development. In B. R. Worthen & J. R. Sanders (Eds.), *Educational evaluation: Theory and practice* (pp. 150–154). Belmont, CA: Wadsworth Publishing Company. (Reprinted from *Evaluation comment*, pp. 2–7, by M. C. Alkin, 1969, Los Angeles, CA: Center for Study of Evaluation)

Altschuld, J. W. (2005). Certification, credentialing, licensure, competencies, and the like: Issues confronting the field of evaluation. *Canadian Journal of Program Evaluation, 20*(2), 157–168.

Altschuld, J. W., & Engle, M. (Eds.). (1994). *New Directions in Program Evaluation: No. 62. The preparation of professional evaluators: Issues, perspectives, and current status.* San Francisco, CA: Jossey-Bass.

Altschuld, J. W., Engle, M., Cullen, C., Kim, I., & Macce, B. R. (1994). The 1994 directory of evaluation training programs. In J. W. Altschuld & M. Engle (Eds.), *New Directions in Program Evaluation: No. 62. The preparation of professional evaluators: Issues, perspectives and current status* (pp. 71–94). San Francisco, CA: Jossey-Bass.

Altschuld, J. W., & Watkins, R. (in press). A primer on needs assessment: More than 40 years of research and practice. In J. W. Altschuld & R. Watkins (Eds.), *New Directions for Program Evaluation: No. 144. Needs assessment: Trends and a view toward the future.* San Francisco, CA: Jossey-Bass.

Guba, E. G. (1978). *Toward a methodology of naturalistic inquiry in educational evaluation* [Monograph Series, No. 8]. Los Angeles: CA: Center for the Study of Evaluation.

King, J. A., & Podems, D. (Eds.). (2014). Professionalizing evaluation: A global perspective on evaluator competencies [Special issue]. *Canadian Journal of Program Evaluation, 28*(3).

Kirkpatrick, D. L. (1954) *Evaluating human relations programs for industrial foreman and supervisors* (Unpublished doctoral dissertation). University of Wisconsin, Madison.

Lysaght, R. M., & Altschuld, J. W. (2000). Beyond initial certification: The assessment and maintenance of competency in professions. *Evaluation and Program Planning, 23*(1), 95–104.

McDavid, J. C., & Huse, I. (2006). *Literature review: Professionalization of evaluators.* Paper prepared for the CES Evaluation Professionalization Project. Canadian Evaluation Society, Renfrew, Ontario.

McGuire, M., & Zorzi, R. (2005). Evaluator competencies and professional development. *Canadian Journal of Program Evaluation, 20*(2), 73–99.

Patton, M. Q. (1980). *Qualitative evaluation and research methods.* Newbury Park, CA: Sage.

Patton, M. Q. (1982). *Practical evaluation.* Newbury Park, CA: Sage.

Scriven, M. (1973). The methodology of evaluation. In B. R. Worthen & J. R. Sanders. (Eds.), *Educational evaluation: Theory and practice* (pp. 60–103). Belmont, CA: Wadsworth Publishing Company. (Reprinted from *Perspectives of curriculum evaluation* [AERA Monograph 1], pp. 39–83, by R. Tyler, R. Gagne, & M. Scriven, 1967, Chicago, IL: Rand McNally and Company)

Stake, R. E. (1973). The countenance of educational evaluation. In B. R. Worthen & J. R. Sanders. (Eds.), *Educational evaluation: Theory and practice* (pp. 106–124). Belmont, CA: Wadsworth Publishing Company. (Reprinted from *Teachers College Record*, pp. 523–540, by R. E. Stake, 1967, New York, NY: Teachers College Columbia University)

Stevahn, L., King, J., Ghere, G., & Minnema, J. (2005). Establishing essential competencies for evaluators. *Canadian Journal of Program Evaluation, 20*(2), 101–123.

Stufflebeam, D. L. (1973). An introduction to the PDK book: Educational evaluation and decision making. In B. R. Worthen & J. R. Sanders (Eds.), *Educational evaluation: Theory and practice* (pp. 128–137). Belmont, CA: Wadsworth Publishing Company. (Reprinted from *Educational evaluation and decision-making*, by D. L. Stufflebeam, 1971, Itasca, IL: F.E. Peacock Publishers)

Witkin, B. R. (1984). *Assessing needs in educational and social programs: Using information to make decisions, set priorities, and allocate resources*. San Francisco, CA: Jossey-Bass.

Worthen, B. R. (1994). Is evaluation a mature profession that warrants the preparation of evaluation professionals? In J. W. Altschuld & M. Engle (Eds.), *The preparation of professional evaluators: Issues, perspectives, and programs* (pp. 3–16). San Francisco, CA: Jossey-Bass.

Worthen, B. R., & Sanders, J. R. (1973). *Educational evaluation: Theory and practice*. Belmont, CA: Wadsworth Publishing Company.

JAMES W. ALTSCHULD *is professor emeritus at the College of Education and Human Ecology, The Ohio State University.*

MOLLY ENGLE *is a professor at the College of Education and evaluation specialist at Oregon State University Extension Service.*

King, J. A., & Stevahn, L. (2015). Competencies for program evaluators in light of adaptive action: What? So what? Now what? In J. W. Altschuld & M. Engle (Eds.), *Accreditation, certification, and credentialing: Relevant concerns for U.S. evaluators. New Directions for Evaluation, 145,* 21–37.

2

Competencies for Program Evaluators in Light of Adaptive Action: What? So What? Now What?

Jean A. King, Laurie Stevahn

Abstract

This chapter considers next steps in the development and use of evaluator competencies in the United States and globally. It begins with a brief grounding in definitions, then applies the framework of adaptive action (Eoyang & Holladay, 2013), asking "What?" to first describe the current status of evaluator competencies, "So what?" to discuss the implications of that status, and finally "Now what?" to identify potential actions that might attend to the complexity of change in the field of evaluation. © Wiley Periodicals, Inc., and the American Evaluation Association.

T he time has come at last for the field of program evaluation in the United States to address head-on an issue that scholars and the leaders of professional evaluation associations have discussed periodically for over 30 years: What is the set of competencies that an individual must have to conduct high-quality program evaluations? In an assessment of the professional status of program evaluation 20 years ago, Worthen (1994) acknowledged the existence of evaluation's unique set of knowledge and skills, but at that time discussion in the field centered either around individuals' anecdotal lists (Kirkhart, 1981; Mertens, 1994; Patton, 1990;

Scriven, 1996) or the reasons why the field's diversity made the development of a common list of competencies impossible (Smith, 1999).

For a team of four Minnesotans (two of whom are coauthoring this chapter), the impetus to develop a set of evaluator competencies grew from the developers' experiences in fields that had successfully created sets of competencies. If other fields could develop competencies, then why not program evaluation? In contrast to other fields that frequently use a formal process like job analysis or a competency study using behavioral event interviews (Spencer & Spencer, 1993) to develop competencies (Wilcox & King, 2014), the team that developed the Essential Competencies for Program Evaluators (ECPE) used a more inductive one detailed in Wilcox (2012). They read previous writing about evaluator competencies, examined evaluation textbooks, reflected on their personal experience in the field, and eventually conducted a multi-attribute utility analysis with a small yet comprehensive snowball sample of local evaluators and evaluation students (King, Stevahn, Ghere, & Minnema, 2001). After the creation of initial competencies, they spent another four years revising them, conducting a painstaking and time-consuming crosswalk of the initial set with other standard-setting documents: the *Program Evaluation Standards* (Joint Committee on Standards for Educational Evaluation, 1994); the *Guiding Principles* (American Evaluation Association, Task Force on Guiding Principles for Evaluators, 1995); and the *Essential Skills Series* (Canadian Evaluation Society [CES], 1999).

With the publication of the ECPE almost 10 years ago, the question of *whether* the field could develop evaluator competencies was functionally answered, and the answer was yes. Since that time, a number of people and groups have used the ECPE in a variety of settings. Evaluators and their professional associations in countries such as South Africa and Aotearoa New Zealand have created context-specific sets of competencies based in part on the ECPE, and three countries—Canada, Japan, and Thailand—have gone even farther and established procedures to credential evaluators (Kuji-Shikatani, Chapter 5 of this issue).

The purpose of this chapter is not to raise yet again the existential question regarding evaluator competencies, but rather to consider next steps in their development and use both in the United States and globally. We begin with definitions to be clear about exactly what we mean when we discuss competencies. Next, we move to the process of adaptive action (Eoyang & Holladay, 2013), which is well suited to understanding because, in situations where uncertainty abounds, adaptive action asks three simple questions: "What?" "So what?" and "Now what?" We address each of these in turn. The first requires thoughtful observation of a situation; the second, a discussion of possible options and their implications; and the third, a list of potential next steps. We then conclude with thoughts on appropriate actions regarding the future of competencies for program evaluators. We

New Directions for Evaluation • DOI: 10.1002/ev

believe it is time for the field of program evaluation to take action that attends to the revision and use of competencies.

Definitions, Distinctions, and Intersections Regarding Competencies

It is helpful to have clear definitions of terms commonly used in discussing this topic: knowledge, skills, and dispositions; competencies; and competence. The first three are the stuff of basic curriculum development, that is, what a person can learn (knowledge), what a person can do (skill), and the way that a person can think or feel about something (disposition or attitude) (McLagan, 1997; Posner & Rudnitsky, 2005).

The distinction between the second and third terms on the list—between competencies and the broader notion of competence—is technically important. *Competence* is the "habitual and judicious use of communication, knowledge, technical skills, clinical reasoning, emotions, values and reflection in daily practice for the benefit of the individual and community being served" (Epstein & Hundert, 2002, p. 226). By contrast, the requirements for *competencies* are knowledge, skills, and attitudes that are applied and observable (Schoonover Associates, 2003), specific practices related to particular knowledge, skills, or dispositions. Competencies are a

> ... set of related knowledge, skills, and attitudes that enable an individual to effectively perform the activities of a given occupation or job function to the standards expected in employment. (Richey, Fields, & Foxon, 2001, p. 31)

As Wilcox and King (2014) note, if one uses this definition of competency, what are labeled "competencies" in the ECPE do not create a set of competencies *per se*, but an outline of evaluator competence. While this distinction is important in some circles, the pragmatic use of the existing ECPE suggests that in the field of evaluation, it may not be. We therefore will continue to use the term *competency* to label general knowledge, skills, and dispositions rather than the applied versions of the same.

As further conceptual grounding for this discussion, Figure 2.1 contains an important detail of what Scriven labels the transdiscipline of evaluation (Coryn & Hattie, 2006; Scriven, 1991). Except in those situations when evaluation itself is being studied, whenever an evaluator conducts a study, there is always specific content to address; programs focus on particular subjects or combinations of subjects (teen pregnancy, juvenile recidivism, early childhood literacy, shared governance, or any of an extensive number of other topics). Evaluator competencies live in the circle labeled evaluation-specific knowledge, skills, and dispositions, but overlap between those and the specific topics the program addresses. That is, the particular competencies for conducting evaluations in that subject may have unique

Figure 2.1. Overlap of Evaluation-Specific and Content-Specific Knowledge, Skills, and Dispositions

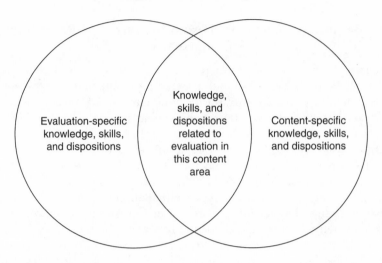

characteristics related to that content. Consider, for example, the practice of evaluation in precollegiate educational evaluation in the era of No Child Left Behind with its common core curriculum versus evaluation in public health or international development programs, where the content would be dramatically different.

The Venn diagram in the figure indicates a challenge for creating a set of general evaluator competencies: the evaluation of certain types of programs may require specific knowledge, skills, and dispositions. There are examples of evaluator competencies that attend to the overlap: (a) the International Board of Standards for Training, Performance and Instruction (ibstpi, 2006) evaluator competencies developed by and for HRD professionals for use in organizations (Russ-Eft, Bober, de la Teja, Foxon, & Koszalka, 2008); (b) the sector-specific example of the measurement and evaluation competencies in support of the AIDS response (Fletcher, Peersman, Bertrand, & Rugg, 2014); and (c) the sets of competencies used to credential educational evaluators in Japan (Sasaki & Hashimoto, 2012) or Thailand (Gauh, 2004; Roengsumran, 2007). The evaluation field, however, has not yet attended to the question of whether and, if so, how evaluator competencies should address subject-specific content.

What? What Is the Current Status of Competencies for Program Evaluators?

In thinking about this current status, we find it helpful to divide the discussion between the conceptual and the practical, labeled here as theory and practice. For clarity, these will be discussed separately, although ultimately any way forward must necessarily attend to both.

Theory

Three conceptual issues arise in considering the current status of evaluator competencies: (a) available validity evidence for existing sets of competencies, (b) the likely importance of context in the further development of competencies, and (c) the expectation that using competencies should lead to or be connected with high-quality evaluation practice.

Validity evidence. First and thankfully, there is initial validity evidence for three of the current sets of competencies. To frame a discussion of competencies for qualitative evaluation, Stevahn and King (2014) compared taxonomies of competencies, including the ECPE, the competencies upon which the CES Credentialed Evaluator (CE) program is based, and the set developed by the International Board of Standards for Training, Performance and Instruction (ibstpi, 2006; Russ-Eft et al., 2008). Table 2.1 summarizes the processes used to generate validity evidence for the three sets, leading to positive validity arguments that support them.

Table 2.2 contains the common content in five areas across these three taxonomies: professional, technical, situational, management, and interpersonal. While specific competencies may differ and more formal validation may be desirable, the fact that these taxonomies share overarching categories is a form of face validity for them. These five categories appear to make sense to practicing evaluators who are developing sets of competencies and provide solid ground upon which to build.

Context. Second, in thinking about competencies, the field of evaluation cannot ignore the potentially powerful effect of context highlighted in Figure 2.1, subject area content. The importance of evaluation context has been emphasized in recent years (Rog, Fitzpatrick, & Conner, 2012), pointing to the likely need to attend to specific content areas when framing competency schemes. The country case examples that contrast, for example, competency activity in South Africa (Podems, Goldman, & Jacob, 2014) and Russia (Kuzman & Tyzgankov, 2014) are evidence of contextual effects on this work.

To address the relationship between evaluation and content, Wilcox (2012) interviewed experienced evaluators in three distinct subject areas, selecting evaluators from public health, education, and nonprofit practice to see if they would respond to competencies differently. The results suggested that those evaluators working in public health and nonprofits viewed the distinction between the content areas of their practice as less important than the roles they played in their organizations. What mattered to them, regardless of content, was the distinction between those working as internal employees and those functioning as external consultants. Conversely, the educational evaluators labeled themselves a distinct group of practitioners,

Table 2.1. Comparison of Validation Processes Across Three Evaluator Competency Taxonomies

Taxonomy	Essential Competencies for Program Evaluators (ECPE) (Stevahn et al., 2005a; also see King et al., 2001)	Competencies for Canadian Evaluation Practice (CES, 2013)	Evaluator Competencies (ibstpi, 2006; Russ-Eft et al., 2008)
Validation process	King et al. (2001): • Multi-Attribute Consensus Reaching (MACR) process generated quantitative and qualitative input on the perceived importance of the competencies for evaluators. • Purposive snowball sample ($N = 31$) of people involved in program evaluation in the greater Minneapolis-St. Paul region in Minnesota, USA, who represented diversity across a range of demographic characteristics. Stevahn et al. (2005a): • Additional systematic qualitative input from evaluation professionals and graduate students ($N > 100$) in formal contexts (i.e., evaluation association conference sessions, university courses, professional development workshops, and consultations with the AEA competencies task force leader) on competency additions, revisions, and deletions. • Crosswalk comparison of the competencies to the Joint Committee Program Evaluation Standards (1994), AEA Guiding Principles (1995), and CES (1999) Essential Skills Series.	• Proposed competencies adapted from ECPE (Stevahn et al., 2005a). • Crosswalk comparison of the proposed competencies to the CES Essential Skills Series (2007/1999), CES Core Body of Knowledge (2002), Treasury Board of Canada Secretariat Competencies for Evaluators in the Government of Canada (2002), Joint Committee Program Evaluation Standards (1994), AEA Guiding Principles (1995), and United Nations Evaluation Group Core Competencies for Evaluators (2007). • CES members surveyed to obtain input on proposed competencies (2008). • CES chapter-based consultations to obtain further input on proposed competencies (2009). • CES approved competencies and adopted the Professional Designations Program to credential evaluators (2009).	Russ-Eft et al. (2008): • Survey generated quantitative input (Likert-scale ratings on the perceived importance of the competencies for one's work) and qualitative input (what should be added or reworded and general comments). • Sought worldwide input from those involved in evaluation practice. Contacted more than 40 professional training and evaluation associations internationally; academic evaluation training programs in several countries, professional networks and listservs, worldwide contacts of ibstpi board members, and those visiting the ibstpi website. • Respondents ($N = 443$) represented considerable diversity across a range of demographic characteristics (i.e., education, gender, age, organizational work settings/contexts, fields of expertise, evaluator role, years in evaluation, evaluation training/courses, membership in evaluation associations, geographic regions for evaluation work).

Source: Adapted from Stevahn & King (2014).

Table 2.2. Cross-Comparison of Evaluator Competency Taxonomies

Common core competency domains (similarities across taxonomies)	Essential Competencies for Program Evaluators[a] (Stevahn et al., 2005a; also see King et al., 2001)	Competencies for Canadian Evaluation Practice[a] (CES, 2013)	Evaluator Competencies[a] (ibstpi, 2006; Russ-Eft et al., 2008)
Professional Focus Acts ethically/reflectively and enhances/advances professional practice	1.0 Professional practice (1.1–1.6) 5.0 Reflective practice (5.1–5.5)	1.0 Reflective practice (1.1–1.7)	• Professional foundations (1.–5.)
Technical Focus Applies appropriate methodology	2.0 Systematic inquiry (2.1–2.20)	2.0 Technical practice (2.1–2.16)	• Planning and designing the evaluation (6.–9.) • Implementing the evaluation (10.–12.)
Situational Focus Considers/analyzes context successfully	3.0 Situational analysis (3.1–3.12)	3.0 Situational practice (3.1–1.9)	(5.) Demonstrate awareness of the politics of evaluation
Management Focus Conducts/manages projects skillfully	4.0 Project management (4.1–4.12)	4.0 Management practice (4.1–4.7)	• Managing the evaluation (13.–14.)
Interpersonal Focus Interacts/communicates effectively and respectfully	6.0 Interpersonal competence (6.1–6.6)	5.0 Interpersonal practice (5.1–5.10)	(1.) Communicate effectively in written, oral, and visual form (3.) Demonstrate effective interpersonal skills (14.) Work effectively with personnel and stakeholders

[a]Numbered items in parentheses are specific competencies listed in the original taxonomies under the larger evaluator domains.
Source: Adapted from Stevahn & King (2014).

whether they worked internally or externally. Given the limited number of people interviewed, these findings are at best suggestive, but do underline the need to pay attention to the overlapping circles in Figure 2.1. This aligns with the observations of King et al. (2001) where the lack of agreement on competencies occurred most commonly on items specific to certain contexts (e.g., conducting reviews of the literature, demonstrating computer application skills, and updating knowledge in relevant content areas).

Improved practice.   Third, in a different vein from the first two conceptual concerns (perhaps owing to the field's commitment to the use of evidence), some have argued that the competencies developed for program evaluation should in fact be linked to high-quality practice, that is, that people who demonstrate the competencies are good evaluators. Some would see this as "walking the talk" of evaluation (Rowe, 2014).

From this perspective, our field's competencies should systematically and meaningfully identify excellent practice. People who exhibit these competencies at the highest levels should be exemplars, and the use of the competencies should link directly to improved evaluation practice. Given the multiple and varied contexts in which people conduct evaluations, this is a tall order that may require stepping back and using a formal approach to develop new competencies or to revise those currently available (e.g., the job analysis or classic competency approaches previously mentioned). Other fields may be less concerned with "proving" this direct connection to quality practice; a common form of competency validation involves inviting a panel of experts to review and affirm the appropriateness of proposed competencies without necessarily studying their effects. Whether the field of evaluation should—or realistically *can*—construct its competencies based on empirical studies of their effects remains to be seen.

Practice

The current status of competencies for program evaluators also requires discussion of two practical issues: (a) the fact that, regardless of the conceptual underpinnings, people are using or adapting the ECPE in a variety of settings; and (b) the need, after almost 10 years, to update the ECPE, their Canadian counterpart that was used in creating the CE program, or any other existing set of competencies.

Competency applications.   The first practical issue simply documents the fact that, regardless of the conceptual status of the competencies, a thousand evaluator competency flowers appear to be blooming around the world, and evaluators are now discussing and using them in numerous settings:

- A special issue of the *Canadian Journal of Program Evaluation* (Podems & King, 2014) includes case narratives about the development of evaluator competencies in four countries (Canada, Aotearoa New Zealand, Russia, and South Africa) and the sector-specific competency development process of a UNAIDS-led initiative.

- The International Development Evaluation Association (IDEAS; IDEAS Working Group on Evaluation Competencies, 2012) and the United Nations Evaluation Group (UNEG; UNEG, 2012) have developed lists of evaluator competencies for international development evaluators.
- Japan and Thailand have competency training for educational evaluators (Roengsumran, 2007; Sasaki & Hashimoto, 2012).
- A working group of the European Evaluation Society has developed a Voluntary Evaluator Peer Review (VEPR) that could potentially be framed around competencies (EES, 2013), and in April 2014 they and the United Kingdom Evaluation Society (UKES) conducted a workshop to discuss the possibilities of its implementation.
- The International Organization for Cooperation in Evaluation is considering organizing a task force on professionalization, evaluator competencies, and certification (D. R. Podems, personal communication, April 29, 2014).
- The Board of the American Evaluation Association (AEA) voted at its June 2014 meeting to create a task force to consider how AEA might move forward in considering evaluator competencies and other paths to professionalization.

This list, while by no means comprehensive (we apologize for the unavoidable omission of many efforts), points to the future of formal uses for evaluator competencies. Discussions within professional associations that sometimes involve government officials highlight the demand side for such development. Following the lead of Canada and Japan, formal uses may include endorsement or credentialing of some sort, accreditation for evaluator training programs, and, at the outer limit, evaluator licensure.

Less official, more personal use of existing competencies is an ongoing companion to such discussions and applications. Students and novice practitioners can use the ECPE self-assessment (Ghere, King, Stevahn, & Minnema, 2006; available at www.evaluation.umn.edu) to engage in personal reflection about evaluation practice and to discuss what it means to be a professional evaluator. Professional development sessions (King, 2013) and training programs (a certificate program at the University of Wisconsin-Stout) have been structured around the competencies, and professors can use the competencies to design curricula and structure instruction for novice evaluators (see Lavelle & Donaldson, Chapter 3 of this issue). In addition, the competencies may assist the reflection required in implementing the new Program Evaluation Standards on evaluation accountability (Yarbrough, Shulha, Hopson, & Caruthers, 2011).

Competency updates. A second practical concern relates to the continuing need to update competencies as evaluation theory and practice evolve over time. A case in point is the initial work on what eventually became the ECPE actually began in the late 1990s (King, Minnema, Ghere, & Stevahn, 1998, 1999). They were first published in 2001 (King et al., 2001), then revised and published in 2005 (Stevahn, King, Ghere, & Minnema, 2005a). A number of things since then have affected the field that are unavoidably not reflected in the ECPE, including but certainly not limited to the following:

- Explicit focus on the importance and effects of cultural issues in evaluation (AEA, 2011; Yarbrough et al., 2011).
- The continuing growth of evaluation and the rapid expansion of evaluation professional associations in international settings.
- Increasing attention to systems thinking and complexity concepts in the field (Patton, 2013; Williams & Hummelbrunner, 2011).
- The rapid development and spread of technology that allows both evaluators and their clients to collect, record, and transcribe data in innovative ways.

Clearly, any set of competencies will require updating to respond to developments that occur over time, suggesting the need for a means to do so. The CES has a functioning system for credentialing evaluators, providing evidence that a system can both be created and function as part of a professional association. Updating competencies must be a part of this process over time.

In summary, the current "what" of evaluator competencies includes both conceptual and practical issues. Conceptual concerns relate to validity, the importance of context, and the degree to which competencies should document and lead to high-quality practice as opposed to being an aspirational set of knowledge, skills, and dispositions. Practical concerns include the fact that, for better or worse, evaluators in a variety of settings are now discussing and using competencies and that these competencies need to be regularly changed as theory and practice evolve. We now move to a consideration of "So what" the use of competencies may mean to the field.

So What? What Are the Implications of the Current Competencies Situation?

Each step of adaptive action—a thorough understanding of the situation, its meaning and implications, and then possible actions—is important for fostering grounded reflection on next steps. What does the current situation surrounding evaluator competencies mean? Now that versions of competencies exist, what might evaluators and their professional associations do with them? What collateral mischief might ensue? To consider the possible consequences of moving forward, again it is helpful to divide the discussion between conceptual and practice concerns, while noting that the two cannot finally be separated in any movement forward.

NEW DIRECTIONS FOR EVALUATION • DOI: 10.1002/ev

Theory

First consider the existing sets of competencies themselves. Regardless of who developed them or how, it is unlikely that anyone would disagree that they could benefit from additional developmental work. In thinking about implications, a number of basic questions arise about any given set, including the following:

- Are all of the listed competencies necessary?
- Are there any minimum required competencies?
- Can one person possess all the competencies, and to what degree should he/she?
- Can evaluators acquire the competencies that they do not already exhibit? Are all of the competencies teachable?
- Since evaluation is frequently performed by teams, can or should competencies be a function of team performance, rather than that of one person?
- How can competencies attend to the specifics of evaluation in a given subject area or a specific cultural context? Should they do so?
- How often should a set of the competencies be updated? What is an appropriate process for updating them?
    The field will have difficulty answering the multiplicity of questions related to the *use* of competencies for training, endorsements, credentialing, and licensure until practicing evaluators are confident that the available competencies are appropriate and worth using.

In thinking about uses, conceptual work and research are also needed to identify the multiple ways that the use of competencies could improve the practice of evaluation, whether through individual reflection and action, through the reflective practice of self-organizing professional learning communities or institutional communities of practice, or through training programs explicitly designed around the competencies (Stevahn & King, 2005b). If the field of evaluator competencies is in its relative infancy, so, too, is the companion field of evaluation instruction and education to attain specific learning outcomes.

Practice

When considering the practical implications of the current status of competencies, one can be struck by the extent and intensity of discussions on the topic and wonder if the field is nearing a tipping point that will push it to common consideration of the competencies for program evaluators. Unlike the Program Evaluation Standards, which were created over 30 years ago and have met the rigorous requirements for national approval through the American National Standards Institute (see http://www.jcsee.org/about), the competencies remain in the early stages of development. Any person or group so inclined can create a set of them appropriate to a given context and freely use them for a variety of purposes. On the one hand, this is a positive. Competencies can be adapted to unique contexts and content, and the creativity that surrounds "let a thousand flowers bloom" may generate innovative ideas that can benefit others. On the other hand, such redundancy may be inefficient, leading to different groups recreating similar sets of competencies at potentially considerable cost. Yet such duplication unintentionally also creates opportunities for comparison, providing a form of validation for common competencies across all taxonomies (Table 2.2). Even so, this does not fully address the question of how to validate specific sets of competencies if organizations believe that validation is important.

This is naturally related to the broader implication of whether the field of evaluation can move toward increased professionalism until there is an agreed-upon set of evaluator competencies. But who can or, perhaps more importantly, who *will* orchestrate, manage, and pay for the development and validation of these competencies? If evaluators are committed to increasing the professional status of the field, can they create collaboration across people and organizations to support that happening? Part of that discussion will necessarily include implications, both positive and negative, of moving toward competency-based practice. Building on current interest, should our evaluation community strike while the iron seems hot?

Now What? Where Might the Field of Program Evaluation Go From Here?

If formal competency statements were truly required for the effective practice of evaluation, they would likely have been generated and validated years ago. The fact is that the field has operated since the 1960s with minimal focus on formalizing competencies, let alone their creation, and it is not evident that having competencies in place will necessarily lead to improved practice. One thing, however, remains clear: Competencies are not a magic bullet that will professionalize and improve the field—to mix metaphors—in one fell swoop. But imagine how this change in the field *might* affect thinking about what it means to be an evaluator and how we designate people as evaluators. This discussion of next steps reverses the order of previous sections, beginning with practical concerns and ending with needed research.

Practical Considerations

Three next steps seem appropriate. First, an obvious action is to encourage those responsible to update the existing sets of competencies (CES, 2013; ibstpi, 2006; Stevahn et al., 2005a) to address changes in the years since the sets were formalized. The process for doing so will be dependent on the group responsible, but the need to do so seems evident.

Second, some of what will result from evaluator competencies rests in the hands of individual practitioners and instructors. Informal use of existing sets of competencies will continue and hopefully benefit those who choose to use them. A related action would be to encourage such use through the creation of informal professional learning communities, both in-person and online, either through professional associations or instructional programs.

A third possible action relates to the prescribed use of any of the sets of competencies, which will require formal consideration and decisions of professional associations and/or government agencies wherever they are located. Individuals interested in professionalizing the field of evaluation can identify potential levers for change in their setting, develop a plan, take action, and then conduct developmental evaluation of the use of competencies and the outcomes of the effort. The CES (Kuji-Shikatani, Chapter 5 of this issue) has done just that and is currently evaluating its CE system to determine how to move forward in light of several years of experience with their credentialing process. As noted above, the AEA has created a task force to study broad issues around credentialing and accreditation, and other professional evaluation associations/organizations in countries around the world are moving in a similar fashion. The Australasian Evaluation Society's Evaluators' Professional Learning Competency Framework (AES, 2013) includes suggestions for different stakeholders on how to use the framework in practice. It seems likely that developments in technology that have made possible routine interaction across time zones increase the feasibility of cross-national connections over time.

Theoretical Considerations

Conceptual next steps relate to the need for meaningful research to answer basic questions related to the competencies and their use for different purposes. We believe that a critical action is to conduct research on questions related to three areas:

- *Developing and validating competencies.* This chapter has detailed several conceptual issues related to the development and validation of existing sets of competencies. Formal studies would begin with a description of the job and tasks of evaluator and lead ultimately to competencies related to excellent practice. While such a process would be difficult, its value would stem from its thorough attention to the issue. The question for the evaluation field is whether or not to use a more systematic approach to developing competencies as opposed to what has been done to date. Research using more extensive formal processes may provide additional support for the competencies that are thereby created.
- *Teaching evaluation using the competencies.* It is one thing to identify competencies and quite another to consider how evaluators can or should

acquire them. What are the best ways to attain the knowledge, skills, and dispositions that distinguish high-quality evaluation practice? As mentioned above, so far there is little research that links specific competencies to such practice. Research on the effects of specific approaches to competencies instruction and outcomes would mark a helpful beginning in learning useful ways to teach novice evaluators the competencies that can lead over time to good practice.

- *The effect and effectiveness of competencies in a variety of settings.* A number of topics related to the use of evaluator competencies merit study, including the following: advantages and disadvantages of using evaluator competencies; the effect of context, culture, and setting on the use of competencies; and the broad question of the extent to which accreditation, credentialing, certification, and/or licensure would ultimately be worth the time, effort, and cost.

Given the ongoing challenge of funding to support evaluation research, this suggestion for extensive research in three areas may appear highly daunting, but in its absence, the field may well continue to face ongoing questions regarding the value of evaluator competencies.

As Eoyang and Holladay (2013) write, "It is easy to become paralyzed by uncertainty. . . . It is easy to find creative ways to describe the difficulties and bask in the hopelessness of complex change" (p. 13). We believe there is the potential for this to happen in the field of evaluation surrounding the creation and use of evaluator competencies. Moving beyond paralysis, difficulties, and hopelessness, this chapter has used the framework of adaptive action, asking "What?"—to first describe the current status of evaluator competencies, "So what?"—to discuss the implications of that status, and finally "Now what?"—to identify potential actions that might attend to the complexity of change in the field of evaluation. Let us collectively identify next steps and consider together how to proceed.

References

American Evaluation Association (AEA). (2011). *Public statement on cultural competence in evaluation.* Retrieved from http://www.eval.org

American Evaluation Association, Task Force on Guiding Principles for Evaluators. (1995). Guiding principles for evaluators. In W. R. Shadish, D. L. Newman, M. A. Scheirer, & C. Wye (Eds.), *New Directions for Program Evaluation: No. 66. Guiding principles for evaluators* (pp. 19–16). San Francisco, CA: Jossey-Bass.

Australasian Evaluation Society (AES). (2013). *Evaluators' professional learning competency framework.* Retrieved from http://www.aes.asn.au/professional-learning/pl-resources.html

Canadian Evaluation Society (CES). (1999). *Essential skills series.* Retrieved from http://www.evaluationcanada.ca/essential-skills-series-evaluation

Canadian Evaluation Society (CES). (2013). *Competencies for Canadian evaluation practice.* Retrieved from http://www.evaluationcanada.ca/site.cgi?s=50&ss=8&_lang=en

Coryn, C. L. S., & Hattie, J. A. (2006). The transdisciplinary model of evaluation. *Journal of Multidisciplinary Evaluation, 3*(4), 107–114.

Eoyang, G. H., & Holladay, R. J. (2013). *Adaptive action: Leveraging uncertainty in your organization*. Stanford, CA: Stanford University Press.

Epstein, R. M., & Hundert, E. M. (2002). Defining and assessing professional competence, *JAMA, 287*(2), 226–235.

European Evaluation Society (EES). (2013). *Towards a Voluntary Evaluator Peer Review (VEPR) system for EES—Concept summary*. Retrieved from http://europeanevaluation .org/community/thematic-working-groups/twg-4-professionalization-evaluation

Fletcher, G., Peersman, G., Bertrand, W., & Rugg, D. (2014). M&E competencies in support of the AIDS response: A sector-specific example. *Canadian Journal of Program Evaluation, 28*(3), 103–120.

Gauh, G. (2004). *Development of the certification of external evaluators for school evaluation based on a competency approach* (Unpublished doctoral dissertation). Chulalongkorn University, Bangkok, Thailand.

Ghere, G., King, J. A., Stevahn, L., & Minnema, J. (2006). A professional development unit for reflecting on program evaluator competencies. *American Journal of Evaluation, 27*(1), 108–123.

International Board of Standards for Training, Performance and Instruction (ibstpi). (2006). *Evaluator competencies*. Retrieved from http://ibstpi.org/evaluator-co mpetencies/

International Development Evaluation Association (IDEAS) Working Group on Evaluation Competencies. (2012). *Competencies for development evaluation evaluators, managers, and commissioners*. Retrieved from http://www.ideas-int.org/documents /file_list.cfm?DocsSubCatID=48

Joint Committee on Standards for Educational Evaluation (1994). *The program evaluation standards: A guide for evaluators and evaluation users* (2nd ed.). Thousand Oaks, CA: Sage.

King, J. A. (2013, August). *Essential Competencies for Program Evaluators*. Workshop presented at the Summer Institute of the American Evaluation Association, Atlanta, GA.

King, J. A., Minnema, J., Ghere, G., & Stevahn, L. (1998, November). *Evaluator competencies*. Paper presented at the meeting of the American Evaluation Association, Chicago, IL.

King, J. A., Minnema, J., Ghere, G., & Stevahn, L. (1999). *Essential evaluator competencies*. Minneapolis, MN: Program Evaluation Studies, University of Minnesota.

King, J. A., Stevahn, L., Ghere, G., & Minnema, J. (2001). Toward a taxonomy of essential evaluator competencies. *American Journal of Evaluation, 22*(2), 229–247.

Kirkhart, K. (1981). Defining evaluator competencies: New light on an old issue. *Evaluation Practice, 2*(2), 188–192.

Kuzman, A., & Tyzgankov, D. (2014). The emerging field of evaluation and the growth of the evaluation profession: The Russian experience. *Canadian Journal of Program Evaluation, 28*(3), 87–102.

McLagan, P. A. (1997). Competencies: The next generation. *Training and Development, 51*(5), 40–47.

Mertens, D. M. (1994). Training evaluators: Unique skills and knowledge. In J. W. Altschuld & M. Engle (Eds.), *New Directions for Program Evaluation: No. 62. The preparation of professional evaluators: Issues, perspectives, and program* (pp. 17–28). San Francisco, CA: Jossey-Bass.

Patton, M. Q. (1990). The challenge of being a profession. *Evaluation Practice, 11*(1), 45–51.

Patton, M. Q. (2013). The future of evaluation in society: Top ten trends plus one. In S. Donaldson (Ed.), *The future of evaluation in society: A tribute to Michael Scriven* (pp. 45–62). Charlotte, NC: Information Age Publishing.

Podems, D., Goldman, I., & Jacob, C. (2014). Evaluator competencies: The South African government experience. *Canadian Journal of Program Evaluation*, 28(3), 71–85.

Podems, D., & King, J. A. (Eds.). (2014). Professionalizing evaluation: A global perspective on evaluator competencies [Special issue]. *Canadian Journal of Program Evaluation*, 28(3).

Posner, G. J., & Rudnitsky, A. N. (2005). *Course design: A guide to curriculum development for teachers* (7th ed.). Boston, MA: Allyn and Bacon/Merrill Education.

Richey, R. C., Fields, D. C., & Foxon, M. (2001). *Instructional design competencies: The standards* (3rd ed.). Syracuse, NH: ERIC Clearinghouse on Information and Technology.

Roengsumran, A. (2007). *The validation of competencies for educational evaluators in Thailand*. Unpublished manuscript, University of Minnesota, Minneapolis.

Rog, D. J., Fitzpatrick, J. L., & Conner, R. F. (Eds.). (2012). *New Directions for Evaluation: No. 135. Context: A framework for its influence on evaluation practice*. San Francisco, CA: Jossey-Bass.

Rowe, A. (2014). A good start, but we can do better. *Canadian Journal of Program Evaluation*, 28(3), 121–126.

Russ-Eft, D., Bober, M. J., de la Teja, I., Foxon, M. J., & Koszalka, T. A. (2008). *Evaluator competencies: Standards for the practice of evaluation in organizations*. San Francisco, CA: Jossey-Bass.

Sasaki, R., & Hashimoto, A. (2012, October). *Certified professional evaluators (C.P.E.) programs in Japan in the complex ecology*. Paper presented at the annual meeting of the American Evaluation Association, Minneapolis, MN.

Schoonover Associates. (2003). *FAQ: Competency model building*. Retrieved from http://www.schoonover.com/schoonover-faqs.asp

Scriven, M. (1991). *Evaluation thesaurus* (4th ed.). Newbury Park, CA: Sage.

Scriven, M. (1996). Types of evaluation and types of evaluator. *Evaluation Practice, 17*(2), 151–161.

Smith, M. F. (1999). Should AEA begin a process for restricting membership in the profession of evaluation? *American Journal of Evaluation, 20*(3), 521–531.

Spencer, L. M., & Spencer, S. M. (1993). *Competence at work: Models for superior performance*. New York, NY: Wiley.

Stevahn, L., & King, J. A. (2014). What does it take to be an effective qualitative evaluator? Essential competencies. In L. Goodyear, E. Barela, J. Jewiss, & J. Usinger (Eds.), *Qualitative inquiry in evaluation: From theory to practice* (pp. 141–166). San Francisco, CA: Jossey-Bass.

Stevahn, L., King, J. A., Ghere, G., & Minnema, J. (2005a). Establishing essential competencies for program evaluators. *American Journal of Evaluation, 26*(1), 43–59.

Stevahn, L., King, J. A., Ghere, G., & Minnema, J. (2005b). Using evaluator competencies in university-based evaluation programs. *Canadian Journal of Program Evaluation*, 20(2), 101–123.

United Nations Evaluation Group (UNEG). (2012). *Standards for evaluation in the UN system*. Retrieved from http://uneval.org/document/library

Wilcox, Y. (2012). *An initial study to develop instruments and validate the Essential Competencies for Program Evaluators (ECPE)* (Unpublished doctoral dissertation). University of Minnesota, Minneapolis.

Wilcox, Y., & King, J. A. (2014). A professional grounding and history of the development and formal use of evaluator competencies. *Canadian Journal of Program Evaluation*, 28(3), 1–28.

Williams, B., & Hummelbrunner, R. (2011). *Systems concepts in action: A practitioner's toolkit*. Stanford, CA: Stanford Business Books.

Worthen, B. R. (1994). Is evaluation a mature profession that warrants the preparation of evaluation professionals? In J. W. Altschuld & M. Engle (Eds.), *New Directions for*

Program Evaluation: No. 62. The preparation of professional evaluators: Issues, perspectives and programs (pp. 3–15). San Francisco, CA: Jossey-Bass.

Yarbrough, D. B., Shulha, L. M., Hopson, R. K., & Caruthers, F. A. (2011). *The program evaluation standards: A guide for evaluators and evaluation users* (3rd ed.). Thousand Oaks, CA: Sage.

JEAN A. KING *is a professor in the Department of Organizational Leadership, Policy, and Development and director of the Minnesota Evaluation Studies Institute (MESI) at the University of Minnesota.*

LAURIE STEVAHN *is a professor in the Educational Leadership Doctoral Program in the College of Education at Seattle University.*

LaVelle, J. M., & Donaldson, S. I. (2015). The state of preparing evaluators. In J. W. Altschuld & M. Engle (Eds.), *Accreditation, certification, and credentialing: Relevant concerns for U.S. evaluators. New Directions for Evaluation, 145*, 39–52.

3

The State of Preparing Evaluators

John M. LaVelle, Stewart I. Donaldson

Abstract

This chapter begins with an analysis of the prior status of the preparation of evaluators and what is going on currently in that regard. The varied, noticeably diverse, and growing options for individuals to enter the field are explained with some recent studies highlighted. The discussion goes beyond traditional university-based programs to include those delivered by evaluation associations, distance education, and other mechanisms. One of the conclusions is a recommendation to more fully delve into what is now taking place and to dig more deeply into how evaluators enter the profession. © Wiley Periodicals, Inc., and the American Evaluation Association.

Since the 1960s, the evaluation profession has experienced dramatic growth, development, and institutionalization. Informal inquiry suggests that opportunities for evaluators to practice their craft are plentiful and that the demand outweighs the supply. The number of professional evaluation organizations has grown from 5 in 1990 to 50 in 2007 (Donaldson, 2007; Donaldson & Christie, 2006) to over 150 in 2014, with more than 34,000 members collectively (Donaldson, 2014). In fact, the American Evaluation Association (AEA) reported more than 7,500 members in 2013. The conceptual development of evaluation has been no less impressive on intellectual and professional fronts. These include rich debates on evaluation theory and practice, deliberation on strategies and methodology, discussions on evaluation competencies, and careful consideration of the myriad ways evaluation can contribute to and improve the global community.

Central to this is the belief that the preservice education of evaluators is integral to quality evaluation practice as well as socialization into the evaluation profession (Altschuld & Engle, 1994). Indeed, it has been argued that "the evaluation field's future success is dependent on sound evaluation [education and training] programs that provide a continuing flow of excellently qualified and motivated evaluators" (Stufflebeam, 2001, p. 445) and that evaluators require preparation to create high-quality, meritorious products. The type and format of the education program selected depend on a number of factors such as awareness of where programs exist, perceived and actual costs, geographic mobility, prior education and experience, and employment status. Beyond that, many practicing evaluators participate in professional development workshops offered through national or regional evaluation organizations, training at for-profit institutions, or a graduate-level university-based program. As a result, the preservice education of evaluators has been a recurring topic of interest in the professional literature and has resulted in important theoretical/descriptive works, as exemplified by the periodic publication of education directories (Altschuld, Engle, Cullen, Kim, & Macce, 1994; Conner, Clay, & Hill, 1980; Engle, Altschuld, & Kim, 2006; LaVelle, 2014; LaVelle & Donaldson, 2010; May, Fleischer, Scheirer, & Cox, 1986).

We will use this chapter to contextualize what it means to be an evaluator in the 21st century. Further, we will explore evaluation preparation over time, diverse definitions of "evaluation training programs," possible opportunities for evaluation education, and new directions for research on the education of evaluators.

What Do We Need to Know to Be an Evaluator?

Practitioners and academics alike have struggled with what it means to be an evaluator. Descriptions of evaluation seem to depend on perspectives, values, experiences, and one's professional orientation. For example, some might see evaluation as an ongoing process for investigating and understanding organizational issues (Preskill & Torres, 1999) or as systematic assessment and improvement for understanding the planning, implementation, and effectiveness of programs (Chen, 2005), sometimes oriented to answering specific questions for intended users (Patton, 1997, 2008), or intended to clarify the empirically supported link between program activities and desired outcomes (Donaldson, 2007). Integrating these diverse views, we suggest that evaluation is a disposition and worldview that combines systematic inquiry and analysis techniques with an eye toward answering important and fundamental questions about programs, policies, and interventions such as: "does it work, why does it work, for whom does it work best, and how do we make it work better?" (Donaldson & Christie, 2006, p. 249).

NEW DIRECTIONS FOR EVALUATION • DOI: 10.1002/ev

Evaluators draw heavily from research methods, inquiry techniques, and other forms of data collection and analysis in their work. It would be impossible for evaluators to practice their craft without such methodological expertise; yet, by closely aligning evaluation with inquiry, evaluation runs the risk of being recognized not as a service profession that seeks to improve organizations and programs, but instead as a methods-driven technical profession where anyone with methodological expertise can call themselves an evaluator (Schwandt, 2008). Along similar lines, work by King, Stevahn, Ghere, and Minnema (2001), Stevahn, King, Ghere, and Minnema (2005a, 2005b), Russ-Eft, Bober, de la Teja, Foxon, and Koszalka (2008), Dewey, Montrosse, Schroter, and Mattox (2008), and LaVelle (2014) suggests that methodological expertise is important for evaluation work, but by itself is not sufficient. Evaluators need to acquire additional skills to help fulfill the responsibilities of evaluative work, including interpersonal competence, communicating with clients, negotiating political situations, managing team members, successfully conducting projects, capacity building, context-responsive data displays, responding to requests for proposals, and so forth.

Part of what makes evaluation such an interesting profession is that its practitioners come from many different backgrounds and work in a range of contexts such as health, government, education, policy, development, social welfare, for-profits, and not-for-profits, among others. It might, therefore, be inferred from evaluators' diverse backgrounds and training that many evaluators have also developed context-related content expertise (evaluators who work in public health could bring expertise in epidemiology or health communications, those in education may have knowledge of pedagogy and classroom design, and individuals in public policy may have experience with legislative or policy analysis). In this manner, evaluation can be viewed as a trans-disciplinary field that both draws from and feeds into many different contexts and domains of knowledge. Some might argue that evaluation professionals bring a mastery of the evaluation process to the table and can, therefore, easily flow between multiple work contexts. We agree, but we also believe that there can be a powerful synergy when an evaluator has expertise in both evaluation and another domain of knowledge. Moreover, an experienced professional can play the important role of translator and communicate the value of evaluation to clients in ways they will find accessible. That kind of proficiency is often the result of being mentored, spending time in the field, participating in high-quality education, working collaboratively in a larger team of content experts, or any combination of these experiences.

Evaluation Education Over Time

Gephart and Potter are credited with compiling the oldest evaluation-specific education directory in 1976. This publication is no longer available

NEW DIRECTIONS FOR EVALUATION • DOI: 10.1002/ev

for review, though it has been reported that their paper contained information on 80 evaluation education programs (May et al., 1986). Conner et al. (1980) conducted the next survey of evaluation education programs and reported on a number of curricular variables such as the types of classes offered, internship opportunities, and average enrollment. Conner et al.'s (1980) survey found 67 evaluation programs in the United States, primarily housed in schools of education, educational psychology, psychology, and public policy. Conner et al.'s study described a range of educational opportunities, from single courses in evaluation to structured curricula that were designed to create methodologically strong evaluation practitioners. May et al. conducted the next survey in 1986 and identified 44 programs in the United States and two internationally. That study also found a range of evaluation educational opportunities and evidence of a movement away from individual course experiences and toward more coherent educational experiences with strong curricular structure, sequencing, and specific educational outcomes. Altschuld et al. published the following survey in 1994, illustrating 38 programs in the United States, 10 in Canada, and one in Australia. That investigation made a significant contribution to our understanding of evaluation education programs by beginning to disentangle the evaluation core content (foundations, procedures, theories) from supporting courses, such as inquiry methodology, statistics, needs assessment, and other content areas.

In 2006, Engle et al. reported 27 programs in the United States, six in Canada, two in Australia, and one each in Iceland, Belgium, and the West Indies. The Engle et al. study was valuable because it asked program representatives to specify the importance they placed on specific learning outcomes such as the ability to conduct evaluations, to teach evaluation, and to conduct research on evaluation. Respondents placed the greatest emphasis on the ability to conduct evaluations, as might be expected in such an applied field, but lower emphasis on the ability to either teach evaluation or conduct research on evaluation. This primary emphasis on evaluation practice might lead one to wonder how the next generation of evaluation scholars and professors will be educated and socialized (more on this later).

In 2010, LaVelle and Donaldson reported on 48 programs in the United States, primarily housed in schools of education, using an Internet-based curricular document analysis technique. LaVelle and Donaldson's study demonstrated the utility of using online sources to gather program information, which was not a viable technique until relatively recently, and painted a picture of evaluation education programs that was more consistent with the observed rise of evaluation practice. When examined longitudinally, these data suggest a decline in evaluation education programs spanning from 1980 to 2006 and a recent growth in programs (LaVelle & Donaldson, 2010). This trend might be partly explained by the methods used to conduct the studies—pen and paper surveys versus online surveys versus online document analysis (LaVelle, 2014; LaVelle & Donaldson, 2010)—and changing definitions of "program."

An Evolving Definition of "Program"

Examining evaluation education programs over time has been a challenge because the operational definition of "program" has evolved as the profession has become more nuanced and sophisticated. It is unclear what Gephart and Potter's definition was, and Conner et al. (1980) did not provide a definition for what constituted a program. May et al. (1986) provided the first formal definition, which stated that a "program shall prepare students to conduct independently a program evaluation" (p. 72). Altschuld et al. updated this definition in 1994 by specifying that a program must contain "multiple courses, seminars, practicums, offerings and so on designed to teach evaluation principles and concepts" (p.72). This flexible definition was meant to be interpreted in multiple ways, but purposefully excluded single-course experiences (Altschuld et al., 1994).This definition was later used by Engle et al. (2006) and LaVelle and Donaldson (2010) for their studies, and was recently updated to be even more specific such that curriculum must have two or more courses with the term "evaluation" in the title (LaVelle, 2014). It might be argued that this evolution of more sophisticated definitions reflects the development of the evaluation profession; however, it makes side-by-side comparisons of programs difficult without re-analyzing previous directories (LaVelle, 2014).

Where Might Would-Be Evaluators Receive Preparation?

Today, there are many options for would-be evaluators to receive professional preparation. We identify four broad categories: university programs, professional development workshops, webinars, and on-site training opportunities.

University Programs

University-based evaluation education programs are a ubiquitous form of formal education. They are formally structured to help the participants achieve specific program-level learning objectives (Bilder & Conrad, 1996) and acquire a broad range of evaluation skills and knowledge. These programs can help students bridge levels of knowledge, make connections between "basic" research methods and evaluation, and expand into applied activities such as intern/externships.

Recent research by LaVelle (2014) examined formal university-based education opportunities that included two or more evaluation-specific courses. Results indicated that in 2011–2012 in the United States, there were over 35 evaluation-specific certificate programs, 50 evaluation-specific master's degrees, and 40 doctoral programs with the purpose of preparing future evaluators, complete with a host of supporting inquiry courses and context-specific courses. This represents a significant increase in the presence of formal evaluation education programs offered through institutions of higher education and suggests that, at this point in time, more universities are offering formal paths in evaluation. Consistent with previous research, LaVelle (2014) found that the majority of evaluation education programs and degrees are being offered through departments of education, educational psychology, psychology, and public policy.

In terms of what was being taught, there were some differences across disciplinary homes and degree types. Students enrolled in evaluation-specific master's tracks were generally learning about quantitative research methods and design, intermediate statistics (multiple regression, analysis of variance, etc.), and for some in schools of education, qualitative methods and design (LaVelle, 2014). There was relatively little variability in the evaluation-specific curriculum at the master's level, and it appeared that most students graduated with a somewhat similar evaluation experience, though they would have experienced different content-specific courses depending on the school/department in which they studied.

There was greater variability at the doctoral level, which is not surprising given that doctoral programs are generally more tailored to the interests and needs of the students, and students matriculate for a greater amount of time (national average of seven years). For programs in education, educational psychology, and psychology, evaluation content comprised the greatest proportion of the courses, followed by quantitative methods and design, assessment and testing, and advanced statistics (factor analysis, structural equation modeling, multilevel modeling). Qualitative methodology was highlighted more notably in education. By contrast, for programs housed in public policy, nonevaluation courses were given priority with greatest emphasis placed on policy-specific inquiry techniques, followed by economics/econometrics, evaluation, quantitative design, and lastly intermediate statistics (regression, analysis of variance).

Professional Development Workshops

Professional development workshops provide valuable opportunities for evaluators to refine their existing knowledge and skills or develop new knowledge and skills. Generally, they tend to be offered by national professional evaluation organizations as part of annual conferences (American Evaluation Association [AEA], Canadian Evaluation Society [CES], European Evaluation Society [EES], African Evaluation Association [AfrEA]), regional evaluation affiliates, or universities that provide professional development in addition to normal curricular offerings (Claremont Evaluation Center's Workshop Series on Evaluation and Applied Research Methods).

NEW DIRECTIONS FOR EVALUATION • DOI: 10.1002/ev

For workshops, instructors typically either propose or are solicited to teach a particular topic.

Professional development workshops are generally several days long (AEA series) and consist of workshops or lectures on specific topics. For example, a scan of the AEA's Conference Directories showed a variety of evaluation topics in their professional development series between 2009 and 2013. These topics are designed to help evaluators develop a range of skills, from interpersonal (consulting skills) to analytical (quantitative or qualitative methods) to managerial (contracting). Workshops lasted from three hours of instruction to two days. Sample topics included the following:

- qualitative methods,
- quantitative methods,
- logic models,
- participatory evaluation,
- consulting skills,
- survey construction,
- focus groups,
- politics of evaluation,
- multilevel modeling systems thinking,
- needs assessment,
- mixed methods,
- conflict resolution skills,
- social network analysis,
- data management,
- developmental evaluation,
- program planning,
- feminist evaluation,
- evaluation contracting,
- theory-driven evaluation,
- data displays,
- capacity building,
- quasi-experimental design,
- logic of evaluation,
- utilization focused evaluation,
- geographic information systems, and
- evaluation dissertation proposal writing.

Webinar

A rather recent development in evaluation education is the webinar. This can be similar in content and structure to professional development workshops series yet can span the world using the Internet. An organization that has been a leader in providing free evaluation education using webinars is the EvalPartners Initiative (www.mymande.org). EvalPartners has collaborated with organizations like UNICEF, Claremont Graduate University, and the International Organization for Collaboration in Evaluation, among others, to provide a series of e-learning opportunities, particularly focusing on evaluation and evaluators in developing countries' evaluators. For example, EvalPartners and supporting organizations have delivered a series of interrelated webinars focusing on equity-focused and gender-responsive evaluation, emerging practices in international development evaluation, and national capacity development for country-led monitoring and evaluation systems. Other organizations have utilized webinars to provide evaluation education such as the webcasting of AfrEA conference sessions in 2012 and 2014, or AEA's Coffee Break series.

On-Site Training Opportunities

For individuals working for organizations or for those that need to learn evaluation skills very quickly, on-site training can be a helpful solution. If an organization recognizes that expertise is needed in a particular area, such as logic modeling, and it needs this expertise rapidly, it may contract with an evaluator to visit the site and conduct one or more training sessions. The scope and depth of on-site training is difficult to study empirically (especially with regard to quality and applicability), but it seems likely that some organizations use in-house trainings, possibly alongside other professional development opportunities.

Program Delivery: In-Person, Distance, and Blended

Much development has taken place in the ways that evaluation educators and learners can interact, and these interactions may be broadly categorized into three groups of experiences: in-person, distance, and blended.

In-Person

Traditionally, and primarily, instruction is through shared physical space where the instructor and learners interact in real time. This is the classroom experience and what many people mean when they say they are taking a class, workshop, or seminar. The in-person experience has advantages, like the ability to organize the classroom into small groups for an exercise, a session, or the entire term, and using rapid-response feedback to help guide the learners' intellectual and professional development.

Distance

Technological advances have changed the educational playing field, and the in-person classroom experience is no longer the only venue available to educators and learners. Distance education has become more viable with several colleges and universities, such as Harvard, MIT, and Stanford, using online learning more prominently (Neff & Donaldson, 2013). But, along with becoming more accessible, distance education has also become more distinct with student experiences falling into two main types. A *synchronous* approach to distance learning is where the learner is participating in real time and has the opportunity to ask questions of the instructor during the delivery of instruction, as in a synchronous real-time webinar. In this scenario, the educator and learner can interact during a question/answer session, or there might be ways for groups of distance learners to be teamed up to explore a particular exercise or activity. By contrast, an *asynchronous* application is more solitary (watching pre-recorded videos of a lecture or webinar), and learners don't interact in real time with each other or attend any regularly scheduled class sessions. However, even in an asynchronous environment there are still options for interaction, such as email, message boards, and blogs (Neff & Donaldson, 2013).

Distance education in evaluation can provide some interesting ways for participants to maximize their learning experience. In the synchronous distance courses we have conducted, we have observed an interesting set of participant behaviors, namely, that students have the opportunity to engage in concurrent side conversations as instruction is taking place. These conversations would likely not take place in an in-person classroom without being perceived as disruptive, but in an online environment they can add richness to the educational experience by allowing participants to offer personal reflections and support and/or challenge the instructors' assertions.

Blended

A third type of program delivery is a hybrid of the in-person and distance techniques, combining a distance delivery technique with periodic in-person meetings and experiences, either on-site or perhaps at professional meetings/conferences. This combines strong elements of distance instruction with in-person education, but it is important that the in-person part be perceived as valuable enough for participants to invest in the travel.

Our Current Questions About Evaluation Education Programs

Advances in online searches and curricular analyses have afforded researchers much insight into the status and programmatic offerings of evaluation education programs, both formal and informal. Online document analysis has its advantages, such as letting researchers (and prospective students) gather detailed information about programs as from their webpages, student handbooks/bulletins, and the like, and it might be argued that those online sources constitute an educational contract (LaVelle, 2014; LaVelle & Donaldson, 2010). Online document analysis has its limitations, however, and these data sources depend on regular updating. They must, therefore, be analyzed cautiously. Further, it is challenging to determine the regularity of course offerings, the number of students in attendance, program graduation rates, alumni job placements, and the like, making us wonder about the internal processes of these programs. Addressing these topics would require alternative methods, such as interviews with program chairs/coordinators, surveys, or on-site observations. By employing alternative data collection techniques in addition to online analyses, researchers might be able to paint a more complete picture of evaluation education programs.

Additionally, we have questions about how the quality of evaluation education programs might be measured. For formal university-based programs, one approach for determining quality is accreditation at the university level (Western Association of Colleges and Schools or similar organizations) or at the program level (Association to Advance Collegiate Schools of Business or the American Psychological Association). Using accreditation as one measure of quality assumes that the university-based evaluation education programs accept such oversight and perceive this seal of approval as offsetting the effort and preparation necessary for the review. Furthermore, we wonder if it would be most appropriate to assess programs at the profession level or based on their curricular home, such as schools/departments of education assessed by one uniform set of criteria and schools/departments of psychology assessed by another.

Alternatively, evaluation education programs could conduct self-studies demonstrating program alignment to local/national career opportunities, curricular alignment with the competency frameworks now available via AEA, CES, EES, and submitting those documents for outside review. We are not sure if professional evaluation organizations are interested in engaging in this kind of oversight, but we hope that they will take a more active role in the education of evaluators and a greater empirical interest in how programs are preparing future professionals. Whichever approach is used, it will be important that these processes are transparent and conducted in a manner that is consistent with the goal of organizational learning and continuous improvement.

For non-university programs, it is unclear how their educational offerings are monitored for quality. This is not to say that non-university programs are of poor quality, as they often capitalize on the services of excellent evaluators, teachers, facilitators, and content experts. It means only that there is not yet an external association observing them in the same way that formal university programs are periodically reviewed. Looking to the future sustainability of non-university programs, they should consider developing and adopting methods of reviewing the quality of their offerings, especially as many evaluators are looking for ways to enhance their skills and differentiate themselves in a competitive global marketplace.

New Directions for Evaluation • DOI: 10.1002/ev

Last, with an eye toward the sustainability of the profession, we wonder if conversations should take place about the formal goals of evaluation education programs. Engle et al.'s (2006) study showed that preparing graduates to conduct empirical research and teach evaluation was the lowest priority of the evaluation education programs; instead, evaluation practice was the priority. We agree that anyone who graduates from an evaluation-focused program should, at a minimum, be able to conceptualize and conduct evaluations, either individually or as a part of a team. However, we must be careful if programs are prioritizing the practice of evaluation over scholarship and teaching because this can have implications for the pool of individuals able to teach evaluation to the next generation. We hope that more evaluation education programs will purposefully cultivate and support the next generation of scholars and professors of evaluation, that is, individuals who can conduct evaluations and also conduct empirical studies on the evaluation profession itself. Basic research on an applied profession can be difficult to conceptualize, but we look to works by Mark (2008) and Szanyi, Azzam, and Galen (2012) for insights and ideas. We envision a future where practitioners and scholars (both nascent and mature) can work together to help answer practitioners' important empirical questions and support students in the development of theses, dissertations, and other scholarly work.

New Directions for Research on Evaluation Education Programs

Evaluation has made major advances over the past 50 years. There are more universities offering formal evaluation curricula, and there is greater diversity in the kinds of degrees offered. It is also heartening to see that systematic steps are being taken to make evaluation knowledge available to people across the world, especially in the developing world, through collaborations like the EvalPartners Initiative. We envision a day when evaluation knowledge is available to anyone who wants it, not just those who are able to pay for and physically attend a university-based education programs.

By understanding the education system that prepares future evaluation practitioners, researchers, and theorists, we can begin to disentangle the intricate relationships that exist between job skills, competencies, education, credentialing, certification, and accreditation. One way to think about these relationships is linear. One might imagine a scenario where job skills are aligned with competency frameworks, which are, in turn, addressed in education programs and graduates are later assessed through exams offered by a regulatory agency. Another way to envision these relationships is to think of them as an interconnected system where job skills, competencies, education, credentialing, certification, and accreditation influence each other both directly and indirectly. For example, education programs and job skills simultaneously respond to each other and both concurrently influence the credentialing process, which, in turn, impacts the key criteria for accreditation. In either scenario, it is apparent that education plays an important role in the system.

There are still big questions about evaluation education to be answered. For example, much of the research thus far has been focused at the course title level of analysis; however, some course titles might be designed specifically to attract students to enroll, while other titles may give a very macrolevel description of the content. For example, it is difficult to analyze and categorize a course titled *Research and Evaluation Methods*. To what extent (if any) does its content include information on research design, stakeholder engagement, hypotheses and/or evaluation question development, or other aspects of inquiry? An analysis of student learning objectives might paint a different picture of evaluation education courses and programs than course titles. Also, we wonder if the definition of programs as having "two or more courses with the term *evaluation* in the title" is too broad and if a more nuanced definition might be better for understanding complex educational programs. An example of a more complex definition might be that the curriculum must address a certain percentage of the evaluator competencies as required in their country of work to be considered a full program.

A second new direction might be to study the instructors and professors who are teaching the courses, perhaps by conducting interviews or biographical (curriculum vitae) research. Are instructors members of a professional evaluation organization, an affiliate, or a related professional organization? Is evaluation their primary professional and academic identity, or do they see themselves as an expert in a different content area first and as evaluator second? What experience do they have in designing and conducting evaluations, creating and disseminating scholarly work on evaluation theory, methods, context, or professional issues (Mark, 2008) in peer-reviewed articles, conference presentations, or other forms of professional dialogue? In other words, what is the balance between evaluation practice and scholarship in the professoriate? Should the current balance shift more toward either practice or scholarship?

Finally, we believe that evaluation should empirically examine the pipelines that help feed students into evaluation programs. Can we assess prospective students/practitioners/scholars' knowledge and awareness of evaluation as a profession (LaVelle, 2011)? Do we understand how to diversify our educational programs and profession in terms of race, ethnicity, sexual identity, religion, and nationality (Collins & Hopson, 2014)? How might we maximize diversity, outreach, and impact?

Evaluation education has come a long way, and there is still much to be done. We believe that by continuously studying and improving educational programs, the evaluation profession can steer itself into a strong, enduring future.

References

Altschuld, J. W., & Engle, M. (1994). Editors' notes. In J. W. Altschuld & M. Engle (Eds.), *New Directions for Program Evaluation: No. 62. The preparation of professional evaluators: Issues, perspectives, and programs* (pp. 1–2). San Francisco, CA: Jossey-Bass.

Altschuld, J. W., Engle, M., Cullen, C., Kim, I., & Macce, B. R. (1994). The 1994 directory of evaluation training programs. In J. W. Altschuld & M. Engle (Eds.), *New Directions for Program Evaluation: No. 62. The preparation of professional evaluators: Issues, perspectives, and programs* (pp. 71–94). San Francisco, CA: Jossey-Bass.

Bilder, A. E., & Conrad, C. F. (1996). Challenges in assessing outcomes in graduate and professional education. In J. G. Haworth (Ed.), *New Directions for Institutional Research: No. 92. Assessing graduate and professional education: Current realities, future prospects* (pp. 5–16). San Francisco, CA: Jossey-Bass.

Chen, H. (2005). *Practical program evaluation: Assessing and improving, planning, implementation, and effectiveness.* Thousand Oaks, CA: Sage.

Collins, P. M., & Hopson, R. (Eds.). (2014). *New Directions for Evaluation: No. 143. Building a new generation of culturally responsive evaluators through AEA's Graduate Education Diversity Internship program.* San Francisco, CA: Jossey-Bass.

Conner, R. F., Clay, T., & Hill, P. (1980). *Directory of evaluation training.* Washington, DC: Pintail Press.

Dewey, J. D., Montrosse, B. E., Schroter, D. C., Sullins, C. D., & Mattox, J. R., II. (2008). Evaluator competencies: What's taught versus what's sought. *American Journal of Evaluation, 29*(3), 268–287.

Donaldson, S. I. (2007). *Program theory-driven evaluation science: Strategies and applications.* New York, NY: Lawrence Erlbaum Associates.

Donaldson S. I. (2014). Examining the backbone of evaluation practice: Credible and actionable evidence. In S. I. Donaldson, C. A. Christie, & M. M. Mark (Eds.), *Credible and actionable evidence: The foundation of rigorous and influential evaluations* (pp. 3–26). Newbury Park, CA: Sage.

Donaldson, S. I., & Christie, C. A. (2006). Emerging career opportunities in the transdiscipline of evaluation science. In S. I. Donaldson, D. E. Berger, & K. Pezdek (Eds.), *Applied psychology: New frontiers and rewarding careers* (pp. 243–259). Mahwah, NJ: Lawrence Erlbaum Associates.

Engle, M., Altschuld, J. W., & Kim, Y. (2006). 2002 survey of evaluation preparation programs in universities: An update of the 1992 American Evaluation Association-sponsored study. *American Journal of Evaluation, 27*(3), 353–359.

Gephart, W. J., & Potter, W. J. (1976). *Evaluation training catalog.* Bloomington, ID: Phi Delta Kappa.

King, J. A., Stevahn, L., Ghere, G., & Minnema, J. (2001). Toward a taxonomy of essential evaluator competencies. *American Journal of Evaluation, 22*(2), 229–247.

LaVelle, J. M. (2011). Planning for evaluation's future: Undergraduate students' knowledge of and interest in program evaluation. *American Journal of Evaluation, 32*(3), 362–375.

LaVelle, J. M. (2014). *An analysis of evaluation education programs and evaluator skills across the world* (Doctoral dissertation). Claremont Graduate University, Claremont, CA.

LaVelle, J. M., & Donaldson, S. I. (2010). University-based evaluation training programs in the United States 1980–2008: An empirical examination. *American Journal of Evaluation, 31*(1), 9–23.

Mark, M. (2008). Building a better evidence base for evaluation theory: Beyond general calls to a framework of types of research on evaluation. In N. L. Smith & P. Brandon (Eds.), *Fundamental issues in evaluation* (pp. 111–134). New York, NY: The Guilford Press.

May, R. M., Fleischer, M., Scheirer, C. J., & Cox, G. B. (1986). Directory of evaluation training programs. In B. G. Davis (Ed.), *New Directions for Program Evaluation: No. 29. Teaching evaluation across the disciplines* (pp. 71–98). San Francisco, CA: Jossey-Bass.

Neff, K. S., & Donaldson, S. I. (2013). *Teaching psychology online: Tips and strategies for success*. New York, NY: Psychology Press.

Patton, M. Q. (1997). *Utilization-focused evaluation: The new century text* (3rd ed.). Thousand Oaks, CA: Sage.

Patton, M. Q. (2008). *Utilization-focused evaluation* (4th ed.). Thousand Oaks, CA: Sage.

Preskill, H., & Torres, R. T. (1999). *Evaluative inquiry for learning in organizations*. Thousand Oaks, CA: Sage.

Russ-Eft, D., Bober, M. J., de la Teja, I., Foxon, M. J., & Koszalka, T. A. (2008). *Evaluator competencies: Standards for the practice of evaluation in organizations*. San Francisco, CA: Jossey-Bass.

Schwandt, T. (2008). Educating for intelligent belief in evaluation. *American Journal of Evaluation, 29*(2), 139–150.

Stevahn, L., King, J. A., Ghere, G., & Minnema, J. (2005a). Establishing essential competencies for program evaluators. *American Journal of Evaluation, 26*(1), 43–59.

Stevahn, L., King, J. A., Ghere, G., & Minnema, J. (2005b). Evaluator competencies in university-based evaluation training programs. *The Canadian Journal of Program Evaluation, 20*(2), 101–123.

Stufflebeam, D. L. (2001). Interdisciplinary Ph.D. programming in evaluation. *American Journal of Evaluation, 22*(3), 445–455.

Szanyi, M., Azzam T., & Galen, M. (2012). Research on evaluation: A needs assessment. *Canadian Journal of Program Evaluation, 27*(1), 39–64.

JOHN M. LAVELLE *is the director of Operations and External Affairs for the School of Social Science, Policy & Evaluation at Claremont Graduate University and the director of Operations and External Affairs for the Claremont Evaluation Center.*

STEWART I. DONALDSON *is the dean and professor of the School of Social Science, Policy & Evaluation as well as the School of Community and Global Health at Claremont Graduate University and is the director of the Claremont Evaluation Center.*

McDavid, J. C., & Huse, I. (2015). How does accreditation fit into the picture? In J. W. Altschuld & M. Engle (Eds.), *Accreditation, certification, and credentialing: Relevant concerns for U.S. evaluators. New Directions for Evaluation, 145,* 53–69.

4

How Does Accreditation Fit Into the Picture?

James C. McDavid, Irene Huse

Abstract

Since evaluation does not currently accredit preparation programs, the content of this chapter was virtually a blank slate for the authors. Fittingly, they began by reviewing some background literature as to basic terms, what accreditation might entail, and critically parsing out the benefits of doing so. From there they proceeded to examine fields with a kinship to evaluation (accounting, business management, and human resource development) that have implemented systems to provide accredited status for their educational programs. The results have been questionable and led to perhaps unanticipated recommendations for what evaluation should be considering. © Wiley Periodicals, Inc., and the American Evaluation Association.

P rogram or institution accreditation is one approach to professionalizing a field and was a hot topic in evaluation in the 1990s, along with credentialing and certification (Altschuld, 2005). Worthen (1999) provided a seminal article on professionalization in the United States, and Canadian overviews were done by Cousins, Cullen, Malik, and Maicher (2009) and Jacob and Boisvert (2010). A literature review by Huse and McDavid (2006) also noted that accreditation of academic preparation for evaluators has over time been part of the discourse.

Accreditation merits renewed consideration by evaluators because the process may help to establish a reputational advantage and enhance a profession's stature, credibility, and standardization (Beehler & Luethge, 2013; Roller, Andrews, & Bovee, 2003; Zammuto, 2008). Accreditation can provide a competitive edge in marketing, faculty recruitment, and attaining resources (Roller et al., 2003; Trapnell, 2007). Another benefit is "the perception of quality conveyed by the coveted seal or stamp of approval" that can help students, faculty, and employers make educational, teaching, and hiring choices (Stepanovich, Mueller, & Benson, 2014, p. 104).[1] Nigsch & Schenker-Wicki (2013, pp. 671–672) list strategizing, effective management, data collection, faculty quality, openness, and reputation as advantages of accreditation.

Accreditation for evaluation programs is still raised as a possibility (Davies & MacKay, 2014) based upon the experiences of other fields. Cousins et al. (2009) stated:

> It is essential, we believe, to commit to significant advanced legwork in order to develop a solid understanding of the issue and information needs ... a foundation from which unanticipated challenges can be considered, deliberated, and ultimately addressed. (p. 79)

This discussion is limited to accreditation, bypassing details such as evaluation competencies, curricula, types of degrees, and the varieties of programs. The argument is that while accreditation has appeal and positive aspects, it should be approached with caution. Besides the time, resources, and consensus-building needed to design, implement, maintain, and periodically renew an accreditation system (Elliott, 2013; Nigsch & Schenker-Wicki, 2013; Zammuto, 2008), there are pitfalls.

Three disciplines that are somewhat analogous to evaluation have experience with accreditation: business management, accounting, and human resource development (HRD). The similarities consist of (a) not typically involving life-and-limb decisions for clients of practitioners and not generally being subject to government mandates and oversight of accreditation of programs; (b) having internal divides in values, practices, and theories affecting how students are educated; (c) a global dimension necessitating responding to changing cultural, political, legal, and economic contexts; and (d) struggling with regard to competencies (and measuring same in students and practitioners), suitable curricula, definitions of quality, and accreditation processes.

Agreement on the necessary competencies for a field is one of the stumbling blocks for establishing credentialing, certification, or accreditation systems. That issue continues to spark much dialogue (Davies & MacKay, 2014; Podems, 2014; Rowe, 2014; King & Podems, 2014).

In addition, standards for accreditation cannot remain static in an increasingly competitive and turbulent environment inside and outside of educational institutions. After the global financial crisis in 2008–2009, programs in many jurisdictions must adapt to changes in demand and expectations, often with reduced resources.

Many professions that have *credentialing* have not gone as far as accreditation and, even when it is available on a voluntary basis, it may be sought by only a small percentage of schools. Accounting has accreditation available, yet fewer than 10% of programs are accredited (Trapnell & Williams, 2012). And although a growing number of business education programs are becoming accredited due to international competition, many are still not (Trapnell & Williams, 2012). A 2003 attempt to establish an accreditation system for HRD in the United States "died on the vine," with its defunct Internet site (www.hrdaa.org) last updated in 2007 (Zachmeier, Cho, & Kim, 2014, p. 14).

Evaluation has some history of taking preliminary steps in professionalization. In the United States, a feasibility study on certifying evaluators (but not accreditation) was done for the Board of the American Evaluation Association (AEA) in 1996–1997 (Jones & Worthen, 1999; Worthen, 1999). Trochim and Riggin (1996) offered a conceptual map of what would exemplify an accreditation system. Bickman (1997, 1999) advocated for certification and accreditation for evaluation to claim a domain for professional practice. Worthen (1999), however, voiced the scepticism many felt (and still feel) about the AEA taking a leadership role in credentialing evaluators.[2] He suggested that accreditation would be a less divisive *first* step in professionalizing evaluation, before credentialing or certification. But despite the efforts of the AEA's Accreditation Task Force, "somehow the momentum of this effort was lost" (p. 553).

Though there is little research on costs, benefits, and limitations of accreditation (Apostolou, Dorminey, Hassell, & Watson, 2013; Elliott, 2013; Nigsch & Schenker-Wicki, 2013), there are relevant studies of business school accreditation (Elliott, 2013; Heriot, Franklin, & Austin, 2009; Roller et al., 2003) and a body of provocative critiques (Francisco, Nolan, & Sinclair, 2008; Julian & Ofori-Dankwa, 2006; Kuchinke, 2007; Lowrie & Willmott, 2009; McKee, Mills, & Weatherbee, 2005; Pfeffer & Fong, 2002; Stepanovich et al., 2014; Yunker, 2000). Collectively, they can guide evaluation accreditation discussions.

Let us turn to the concepts, principles, and intended benefits of accreditation; reviews of experiences in business, accounting, and HRD; and two conceptual critiques of proceeding down this path. The concluding section offers a summary of lessons learned from other disciplines.

Background: Concepts, Principles, and Intended Benefits of Accreditation

In the United States, there have been several surveys to describe evaluation programs (two or more courses) in universities (Altschuld, Engle, Cullen, Kim, & Mace, 1994; Engle, Altschuld, & Kim, 2006) and, recently, a web-based search by LaVelle and Donaldson (2010) using a similar definition of an evaluation program as the prior two studies. LaVelle and Donaldson (2010) discovered more evaluation programs than Engle et al. (2006) and their work illustrated the range of institutions that offer evaluation programs: Most are in schools of education (60.4%), followed by educational psychology (14.5%), psychology (10.5%), and public policy (8.3%). Over half of these offered specializations at both the master's and the doctoral levels (52.1%). In Canada, a 2009 web-based search for university evaluation programs/courses only came up with 10 programs, of which four were in education and three were in public administration (McDavid & Devine, 2009). In both countries, evaluation programs are dispersed across fields.

In most professions, agreement on competencies and curriculum is a part of the often years-long process leading up to establishing accreditation systems (Kuchinke, 2007; Van Wyhe, 2007b). Defining a field theoretically and practically, and then taking steps to become a profession through credentialing, certification, and possibly accreditation, is a lengthy process.

Professionalization at a Glance: Key Terms and Concepts

Table 4.1 contains key definitions of Altschuld (1999), later adapted by Huse and McDavid (2006), and in a forthcoming article by Halpern, Gauthier, and McDavid (in press).

The Basic Accreditation Process

The time and resources for designing, implementing, and maintaining an accreditation system depend on the nature, scope, and cohesiveness of a field and relationships with the institutions and programs that train individuals seeking entry to the profession. Before an accreditation process can occur, a field must have established an accreditation body that determines the criteria for assessing programs. This is no small feat.

In business and accounting education programs, criteria for accreditation include (a) clearly stated educational missions and goals, (b) systems and resources to achieve objectives, and (c) systems and resources to ensure the identification and implementation of continuous improvements (Trapnell & Williams, 2012). These are linked to appropriate curriculum, faculty qualifications and responsibilities, research expectations, student responsibilities, facilities, and so forth (Beehler & Luethge, 2013; see appendix in Romero, 2008, pp. 253–254: *AACSB Standards for Business Accreditation*). Accreditation standards for the National Association of Schools of Public Affairs and Administration (United States) additionally specify that a program is to "commit to the values of public affairs, administration, and policy and model them in their operations" (NASPAA Standards, 2009, p. 4).

Table 4.1. Definitions of Certification, Credentialing, Licensure, and Accreditation

Terms/Concepts	Meaning	Comments
Credentialing	A set of courses, a program, or other experiences a person must have to receive a credential. Credentials can either be postsecondary programs for which students have earned academic credit or noncredit offerings (The Evaluators Institute is an example of such a credential). Usually done by a professional society.	Does not specify the skill set attained by the person credentialed, only that they have gone through delineated experiences and courses. Tests or exams may be, but generally are not, used for credentialing; instead these are the courses or training experiences that the individual has taken. There does not have to be agreement on a set of core competencies. Credentialing is voluntary, so it does not exclude practitioners who are not credentialed.
Certification	A process by which a person masters certain skills and competencies in a field as assessed by an external body (usually a professional society in the area of consideration).	Most often done through a formal test or set of tests (certification exams) as in accounting, law, medicine, engineering, and so forth. Certifying body may be legally liable for the skills that they designate as being attained by an individual. Certification may have to be periodically renewed, usually (not always) via continuing education.
Licensure	Licenses are awarded by states/provinces, branches of government, and legal jurisdictions. One must have a license to practice the profession, and penalties are assessed for those practicing without a license. Many times the criteria for licensing are the same as certification and are determined by professional societies/groups.	One may be certified but not licensed as in the case of a physician who has passed the necessary medical examinations but is not legally licensed to practice. Licensure is recognized in law—it has the effect of excluding any practitioners who are not legally licensed. Licensing jurisdictions set up review panels in cases where there is malfeasance or unsafe practice. Control of licensure resides outside of the professional group but is almost always highly influenced by it.

(Continued)

New Directions for Evaluation • DOI: 10.1002/ev

Table 4.1. Continued

Terms/Concepts	Meaning	Comments
Accreditation	Accreditation is a mechanism whereby the educational program of an agency or educational institution is assessed by an external panel against established criteria. If it passes review, the program receives a formal document indicating that it is accredited (usually for a fixed time period).	Accreditation reviews typically focus on the institution, faculty, systems, courses, experiences and the processes that comprise or support a program (the context, the inputs, the processes, the outputs, and the outcomes for a program), and the student competencies that the program or institution is expected to address.

The Council for Higher Education (Eaton, 2012) summarizes the steps (in adapted form below) in a typical accreditation.

- **Self-study**. Using guidelines prepared by the accrediting body, institutions, and programs generates a self-evaluation of their performance, based on accrediting organizations' standards and measures. The self-evaluation is submitted to the accrediting organization.

  - **Peer review**. An accreditation review is conducted primarily by peers in the profession. They examine the self-study and serve on visiting teams that review programs. Peers constitute the majority of members of the accrediting commissions or boards that make judgments about accrediting status.
  - **Site visit**. Accrediting organizations normally send a visiting team to a program. The self-study is the foundation for the team visit. Teams, besides the peers described above, may also include public members (nonacademics who have an interest in higher education). Team members are volunteers and not compensated.
  - **Judgment by accrediting organization**. Accrediting organizations have decision-making bodies (usually commissions) made up of administrators and faculty from institutions and programs as well as public members. Commissions may affirm accreditation for new institutions and programs, reaffirm it for ongoing institutions and programs (full accreditation or provisionally where problems have been identified) or deny accreditation.
  - **Periodic external review**. Programs continue to be reviewed over time (between formal accreditation episodes). They normally prepare a self-study (performance report) and may or may not undergo a site visit each time. Often, recommendations for improvements are tracked for implementation (pp. 6–7).

Few studies have assessed the costs of accreditation (Heriot et al., 2009 and Roller et al., 2003 are exceptions), but the literature does provide indications of the types of costs to be expected. Whittenburg, Toole, Sciglimpaglia, and Medlin (2006) list the following "potential costs of AACSB accreditation" (p. 11):

- Initial and annual AACSB fees...
- Faculty resources...[for] hundreds (if not thousands) of hours of faculty hours [for] preparation for AACSB accreditation.
- Increased need for instructional resources...to meet accreditation student/faculty adequacy requirements...
- Increased demand for research resources...to meet academic requirements for accreditation.

Heriot et al. (2009) note that "schools seeking initial accreditation may need to change programs, curricula, staffing, administration, and facilities" (p. 283). In their study of 10 American business schools that had gone through the AACSB accreditation process, one-time costs were for consultants, a mock review, the peer-review team, and infrastructure upgrades. Annual costs include "faculty salaries, recruitment, technology, professional development, library holdings and information access, [and] AACSB International dues and conference participation" (p. 286). Expenditures of course depend on the individual circumstances of a school.

Intended Benefits of Accreditation

The benefits of accreditation systems can accrue to students, faculty, employers, clients, the profession, and institutions. Roller et al. (2003) observed that accreditation gives a degree of confidence that a program "meets or exceeds minimum standards of excellence," has "a uniformity of educational standards," and "helps high quality students identify high quality programs" (p. 197). Trapnell (2007) highlighted the transparency that can help students make choices. A profession may benefit from accreditation by building cohesion and attaining status in its competition with other disciplines. Van Wyhe (2007b) states, "In search of the status of law and medicine, accounting professionals began in 1937 to press for schools of accounting and also for accreditation" (p. 497).

Other benefits are the development of networks and alliances, enhanced reputation and legitimacy, and greater incentives for program and school improvement (Beehler & Luethge, 2013; Elliott, 2013; Everard, Edmonds, & Pierre, 2013; Romero, 2008). These can be useful for marketing accredited programs and schools, a feature highlighted by proponents (Beehler & Luethge, 2013; Romero, 2008; Trapnell, 2007; Zammuto, 2008).

Experiences in Initiating and Launching Accreditation: Examples From the Fields of Business, Accounting, and Human Resource Development

Accreditation involves agreement on the professional association(s) comprising the accreditation body, funding, standards to be achieved and maintained by accredited institutions, program eligibility requirements, and how to make ongoing changes to the accreditation system. In business management, accounting, and HRD, challenges have been evident in these areas; below are some that resonate with evaluation.

Business Management

The first accrediting body for business management education was the American Assembly of Collegiate Schools of Business, now the Association to Advance Collegiate Schools of Business (AACSB) International. It was founded in 1916, by 16 institutions (of 30 at the time; Zammuto, 2008) to advance the quality of management education. The AACSB was the only such accreditation association until 1988, after which four more were started (Zammuto, 2008). The impetus for their launch was rigid standards and perceived inflexibility in the face of diverse and variously sized programs and institutions (Roller et al., 2003).

The initial emphasis was on universal standards: criteria were specified for inputs, program processes and content, and outputs such as quality of research publications by faculty and achievements by students. Since 1991, the focus has shifted to strategic alignment with self-selected outcomes, perhaps driven by remaining competitive with the new accreditation bodies entering the scene (Lowrie & Willmott, 2009; Yunker, 2000). This change has been controversial (Everard et al., 2013; Francisco et al., 2008; Lowrie & Willmott, 2009; Van Wyhe, 2007b; Yunker, 2000).

The AACSB has had explosive growth internationally (Trapnell & Williams, 2012). In the United States, over half of all business schools have accreditation from one or more of the three U.S.-based accreditation bodies (Zammuto, 2008), and the numbers may have resulted in dilution of the perceived quality and credibility of the AACSB "seal of approval" (Francisco et al., 2008). For evaluation, the changes in the business education accreditation processes illustrate what could happen. Even if consensus is achieved, institutionalization of standards and processes may have negative effects in the future (David, 1985).

Accounting

Van Wyhe (2007a, 2007b) details the history of accounting professionalization efforts in the United States since the early 1900s. Despite attempts by the American Institute of Certified Public Accountants (AICPA) to establish an accrediting body, in the end it was the AACSB that became the main one for accounting education (Van Wyhe, 2007b). Accounting education is usually in business schools, and its "professional enculturation" is relevant to evaluation (see Chelimsky, 2013; Cousins, 2013; Fetterman & Wandersman, 2005; House, 2011; Patton, 2008).

From the start, there was an accreditation-related disagreement within the AICPA's Board on Standards for Programs and Schools of Professional Accounting about the length of programs (four vs. five years). In 1976, an alternative committee recommended that "[p]rofessional preparation would include the traditional accounting subjects as well as the organization of the profession, ethics, and the environment of accounting" (Van Wyhe, 2007b, p. 484). Further it stated that much of the faculty should have practical experience, so that the curriculum could "stress realism, through the use of cases and practical matters" (p.484). However, disagreements prevailed, and in 1978 the AACSB announced that it would be accrediting accounting programs. The AACSB standards differed from those of AICPA, but "now the business school deans of the AACSB were directing the process," with a "demand for rigorous quantitative research from faculty, and … less emphasis on practice and professionalism" than desired by the AICPA (p. 486). Debates raged among academics and practitioners, particularly in the hours of schooling necessary. It was not clear whether the disagreements were based on competition between professional bodies or views of how to improve accounting education (Van Wyhe, 2007a, 2007b).

Accounting and evaluation are different, but the question is *why* a field decides to include accreditation as part of its professionalization. In accounting, stature seemed to play a greater role than improving education for the benefit of students, faculty, employers, and clients.

Human Resource Development

More than business or accounting, HRD—like evaluation—is a field of study and practice, and is a discipline still defining itself (Stewart & Sambrook, 2012; Worthen, 1999; Zachmeier, Cho, & Kim, 2014). Pedagogical diversity in HRD in the United States echoes evaluation. The United Kingdom's HRD education system has a more centralized human resource *management* focus and a more business-centric, managerial training approach (Kuchinke, 2003). This may explain why the United States failed to maintain the accreditation system begun in 2003 (Zachmeier et al., 2014), whereas the United Kingdom's accreditation system is ongoing (Kuchinke, 2003). In the United Kingdom, there is a division between HR academia, which focuses on human resource *development*, and HR practice, which stresses human resource *management* for organizations (Stewart & Sambrook, 2012). The debate is between academic learning as opposed to more performance based activity—a debate similar to evaluation (Alkin, 2004, 2013).

Where an HRD program is housed affects the curriculum offered. Zachmeier et al. (2014) studied programs in the United States and determined that 48 (44%) were in schools or colleges of education and 28 (30%) in schools or colleges of business (with the remainder in technology, arts and sciences, professional studies, etc.). In the United Kingdom, most HRD programs are in business, with a distinct managerial approach in the curriculum (89%; Kuchinke, 2003). Kuchinke, using a different methodology, found that for the United States, the figure was 76% in schools of education. For the United Kingdom, the Chartered Institute of Personnel and Development (CIPD) accredits HRD educational institutions (Kuchinke, 2003), and the HRD professional associations and accreditation and certification systems are strongly linked to the nation's regulatory bodies and education system. The United States is more decentralized with linkages "notably absent" (Kuchinke, 2003, p. 290). Despite the distinctions, in both countries little of the hiring of HRD practitioners shows concern for either certification or accreditation (Cohen, 2012; Kuchinke, 2003).

Dooley (2005), in "Accreditation, or Standards for Academic Programs?," noted "[t]his issue has been debated [in the U.S.] and discussed for as long as the Academy [of Human Resource Development, founded in 1993] has been in existence" (p. 299). Zachmeier et al. (2014) observed that by 2007 the Human Resource Development Accreditation Association failed to maintain an accreditation system. Like evaluation education, HRD has experienced growing numbers of programs internationally, and the diversity of the field makes it difficult to professionalize in the United States (Zachmeier et al., 2014) and, to a lesser extent, in the United Kingdom (Stewart & Sambrook, 2012).

In summary, the experiences in business, accounting, and HRD education suggest:

- the more diverse a field, the more difficult it is to achieve consensus on competencies, curricula, certification, and accreditation;
- most accreditation system initiatives take decades of work and negotiation within the professional bodies of the field;
- while there are benefits for the quality and credibility of programs and institutions, the process can become diluted over time as more programs and institutions enter the accreditation fray;
- accreditation is costly and it is difficult to assess the balance of costs and benefits; and
- in non-health-related fields, even where *credentials* are important to employers, accreditation of institutions is often not a large factor in hiring, and many credentials originate from nonaccredited programs or institutions.

Critical Perspectives on Accreditation: Applying Institutionalist and Critical Theory Lenses

Accreditation systems are complex (Elliott, 2013; Francisco et al., 2008; Julian & Ofori-Dankwa, 2006; Heriot et al., 2009; Nigsch & Schenker-Wicki, 2013) and, if instituted, schools might need to change programs, curricula, admissions standards, staffing, administration, or facilities. Beyond that, ongoing efforts will be needed to sustain momentum for periodic review and reaccreditation (Elliott, 2013).

Now we outline critical assessments of accreditation, as related to evaluation, through two lenses: institutional/organizational and critical theories. Stepanovich et al. (2014) suggested a third one (systems theory), which is incorporated into the institutional/organizational lens.

Institutionalist Forces: Professional Parameters and the Search for Legitimacy

Organizational theory posits that the drive to achieve or maintain legitimacy, resources, and stability may create pressures to adopt or imitate formal rules or structures that may be strategically relevant or may be symbolic and can hinder an organization's effectiveness (DiMaggio & Powell, 1983; Feldman & March, 1981; Meyer & Rowan, 1977). Formalized institutional pressures can inhibit innovation and diversity in a field, hamstringing flexibility and creating a culture of control and compliance rather than of creativity (Julian & Ofori-Dankwa, 2006; Thomas, Billsberry, Ambrosini, & Barton, 2014). This is relevant in turbulent, uncertain contexts where adaptability is needed to address fast-changing public concerns (Julian & Ofori-Dankwa, 2006; Kuchinke, 2007; Stepanovich et al., 2014), although the flexibility problem is disputed by Romero (2008) and Zammuto (2008). Academic freedom can become stifled as an accreditation process becomes institutionalized (Harvey, 2004). McKee et al. (2005) identify a number of historical concerns about accreditation including the potential for a "cookie cutter approach," with "a loss of control over curricula [and] lack of attention to the ultimate roles of school graduates" (p. 297). Pfeffer and Fong (2002) argue that AACSB accreditation tends to constrain business education and MBA programs into a status quo mode. McKee et al. (2005) state

"organizations are also constrained by the very legitimacies they create and exist within." (p. 291)

Institutionalization-related implications for the evaluation field are:

1. Accreditation may require more time and funding to address qualification standards that are more ritualistic in nature than actually addressing educational effectiveness.

2. Accreditation may breed complacency and inhibit creativity, innovation, and new perspectives in the evaluation field.
3. Accreditation may lock in curricular or structural details that do not address the needs of evaluation students and clients.

Fifteen years ago Worthen, in considering evaluator certification and agreement on competencies, looked at the early 1970s and suggested, "Evaluators back then were much more unified in their views about what evaluation is" (Worthen, 1999, p. 543). Arguably there is now *less* unanimity about the field, and if it had established an accreditation process then would it have the pedagogical and methodological diversity and the reach that it has today?

Critical Theory: Who Makes the Rules and Enforces Them?

The critical theorist lens can be useful for considering *who* determines initial and ongoing accreditation standards and the longer term implications of those choices. Pfeffer and Fong (2002) and Kilpatrick, Dean, and Kilpatrick (2008) pointed out that the business education field's decision to use the analytic, postpositivist paradigm in its accreditation system privileges that paradigm over more holistic views of education (Stepanovich et al., 2014). Kuchinke (2007) noted that some writers "have criticized the predominance of functionalist ideological commitments evident in HRD research and teaching and called for greater inclusiveness of critical and feminist frameworks" (p. 112).

For critical theorists, legitimacy is tied to control and power issues. Lowrie and Willmott (2009) and Kilpatrick et al. (2008) maintained that the "rationality" of an accreditation system encourages stakeholder passivity and leads to bureaucratic responses, a focus on efficiency over effectiveness, and an instrumental, functionalist approach with emphasis on monitoring by using quantified measures.

Initial determiners of accreditation processes can instill a self-perpetuating system, with pressures to conform. An attribute of evaluation is its multidisciplinarity (Cousins et al., 2009). Navarro (2008) in his survey of MBA curricula in U.S. business schools suggested that there was "a lack of emphasis on required multidisciplinary integration and experiential components" (p. 108). Nigsch and Schenker-Wicki (2013) observed that business accreditation changes in the 1990s reflected the wave of New Public Management (NPM) concepts entering academia. Harvey (2004) in his study of higher education in Britain, the United States, and Canada noted that accreditation processes "are not benign or apolitical but represent a power struggle that impinges on academic freedom, while imposing an extensive bureaucratic burden in some cases" (p. 207). Aside from potentially

acting as a restraint on innovation, accreditation "can run counter to peda-
gogic improvement processes" (p. 207). He adds:

> The evidence from the UK and North America shows clearly that accredi-
> tation is just one of a raft of ongoing processes that demand accountability
> and compliance as managerialism continues to bite into academic autonomy
> and undermine the skills and experience of educators. Accreditation is yet
> another layer alongside assessment, audit, and other forms of standards and
> output monitoring (p. 221).

Because "quality" can be nebulous, value-laden factors can be inter-
twined with accrediting programs or schools. Lamenting the U.S. business education system that has been accused of producing students with
"questionable moral compasses" for the past 20 years, Beehler and Luethge
(2013) in discussing accreditation and continuous improvement stated that
"[b]usiness schools worldwide have been criticized for producing MBA
graduates who are strong analytically but weak in skills, such as communication, social responsibility, ethics, and practicality" (p. 282). For evaluation, this can be a cautionary point about setting up a system that focuses
overly on analytics.

Concluding Thoughts

Possible benefits of accreditation include actual and perceived improvements in education programs, transparency, marketing, and distinguishing
a profession (Nigsch & Schenker-Wicki, 2013; Romero, 2008; Zammuto,
2008). On the other hand, establishing an accreditation system is a time-
consuming, expensive, and potentially divisive process, with long-term
consequences (Julian & Ofori-Dankwa, 2006; Kuchinke, 2007; Stepanovich
et al., 2014). Evaluation is characterized by its intellectual ferment about the
purposes of the field, philosophical perspectives that underpin the theories
and the practice of evaluation. New approaches emerge, and they complement or compete with existing ones (see Alkin, 2004, 2013).

Evaluation as a profession (or proto-profession) implies consensus and
a domain for practice, and that is contested. The AEA has the Evaluation
Standards to guide practice, but it has, at best, moral authority for evaluators. The Canadian Evaluation Society credentialing option for evaluators uses the Evaluation Standards and a set of competencies. But to assert
that there is a common understanding of what those competencies mean in
practice is perhaps aspirational. Rowe (2014) is sceptical about institution-
alizing evaluator competencies in Canada: "I expect that any move toward
institutionalization of competencies will expect verifiable, defendable and
easily comparable and accepted mechanisms. Clearly this will favour formal qualifications through academic or professional association venues. I

am not confident this augurs well for evaluation as a practice, although it could certainly improve appearances" (pp. 122–123).

Evaluators have competitors in accountants and management consultants (McDavid & Huse, 2006). For quality and competitive reasons it may be prudent to track the progress of Canada's credentialing system, asking what differences credentialing is making. But based on other fields, evaluation has good reasons for not going down the path of accreditation.

Notes

1. In the United States, the Council for Higher Education and the U.S. Department of Education together recognize accrediting organizations that by 2011 had collectively accredited 7,818 institutions and 22,654 programs (Eaton, 2012).

2. Currently, in the United States The Evaluators Institute (TEI), initiated in 2004, is a principal professional development organization for evaluation. It is affiliated with the AEA and is based at George Washington University, offering several certificates based on combinations of noncredit short courses facilitated by TEI-affiliated faculty.

References

Alkin, M. C. (Ed.). (2004). *Evaluation roots: Tracing theorists' views and influences*. Thousand Oaks, CA: Sage.

Alkin, M. C. (Ed.). (2013). *Evaluation roots: A wider perspective of theorists' views and influences* (2nd ed.). Thousand Oaks, CA: Sage.

Altschuld, J. W. (1999). The case for a voluntary system for credentialing evaluators. *American Journal of Evaluation, 20*(3), 507–517.

Altschuld, J. W. (2005). Certification, credentialing, licensure, competencies, and the like: Issues confronting the field of evaluation. *Canadian Journal of Program Evaluation, 20*(2), 157–168.

Altschuld, J. W., Engle, M., Cullen, C., Kim, I., & Mace, B. R. (1994). The 1994 directory of evaluation training programs. In J. W. Altschuld & M. Engle (Eds.), *New Directions for Program Evaluation: No. 62. The preparation of professional evaluators: Issues, perspectives, and programs* (pp. 71–94). San Francisco, CA: Jossey-Bass.

Apostolou, B., Dorminey, J. W., Hassell, J. M., & Watson, S. F. (2013). Accounting education literature review (2010–2012). *Journal of Accounting Education, 31*(2), 107–161.

Beehler, J. M., & Luethge, D. J. (2013). Achieving success through quality: The role of accreditation and continuous improvement in management education. In A. Altmann & B. Ebersberger (Eds.), *Universities in change: Managing higher education institutions in the age of globalization* (pp. 277–291). New York, NY: Springer.

Bickman, L. (1997). Evaluating evaluation: Where do we go from here? *Evaluation Practice, 18*(1), 1–16.

Bickman, L. (1999). AEA, bold or timid? *American Journal of Evaluation, 20*(3), 519–520.

Chelimsky, E. (2013). Evaluation purposes, perspectives, and practice. In M. C. Alkin (Ed.), *Evaluation roots: A wider perspective of theorists' views and influences* (2nd ed., pp. 267–282). Thousand Oaks, CA: Sage.

Cohen, D. J. (2012). Identifying the value of HR certification: Clarification and more complex models required. *Human Resource Management Review, 22,* 258–265.

Cousins, J. B. (2013). Privileging empiricism in our profession: Understanding use through systematic inquiry. In M. C. Alkin (Ed.), *Evaluation roots: A wider perspective of theorists' views and influences* (2nd ed., pp. 344–352). Thousand Oaks, CA: Sage.

Cousins, J. B., Cullen, J., Malik, S., & Maicher, B. (2009). Debating professional designations for evaluators: Reflections on the Canadian process. *Journal of MultiDisciplinary Evaluation, 6*(11), 71–82.

David, P. A. (1985). Clio and the economics of QWERTY. *American Economic Review, 75*(2), 332–337.

Davies, R., & MacKay, K. (2014). Evaluator training: Content and topic valuation in university evaluation courses. *American Journal of Evaluation, 35*(3), 419–429.

DiMaggio, P. J., & Powell, W. W. (1983). The iron cage revisited: Institutional isomorphism and collective rationality in organization fields. *American Sociological Review, 48*(April), 147–160.

Dooley, L. M. (2005). Accreditation, or standards for academic programs? *Human Resource Development Quarterly, 16*(3), 299–300.

Eaton, J. S. (2012). *An overview of U.S. Accreditation.* Washington, DC: Council for Higher Education Accreditation. Retrieved from http://www.chea.org/pdf/Overview%20of%20US%20Accreditation%202012.pdf

Elliott, C. (2013). The impact of AACSB accreditation: A multiple case study of Canadian university business schools. *Canadian Journal of Administrative Sciences, 30*(3), 203–218.

Engle, M., Altschuld, J. W., & Kim, Y. C. (2006). 2002 survey of evaluation preparation programs in universities: An update of the 1992 American Evaluation Association–sponsored study. *American Journal of Evaluation, 27*(3), 353–359.

Everard, A., Edmonds, J., & Pierre, K. S. (2013). The longitudinal effects of the mission-driven focus on the credibility of the AACSB. *Journal of Management Development, 32*(9), 995–1003.

Feldman, M. S., & March, J. G. (1981). Information in organizations as signal and symbol. *Administrative Science Quarterly, 26*(2), 171–186.

Fetterman, D. M., & Wandersman, A. (Eds.). (2005). *Empowerment evaluation principles in practice.* New York, NY: Guilford Press.

Francisco, W., Noland, T. G., & Sinclair, D. (2008). AACSB accreditation: Symbol of excellence or march toward mediocrity? *Journal of College Teaching & Learning (TLC), 5*(5), 25–30.

Halpern, G., Gauthier, B., & McDavid, J. C. (in press). Special issue on the professional designation program in Canada. *Canadian Journal of Program Evaluation.*

Harvey, L. (2004). The power of accreditation: Views of academics. *Journal of Higher Education Policy and Management, 26*(2), 207–223.

Heriot, K. C., Franklin, G., & Austin, W. W. (2009). Applying for initial AACSB accreditation: An exploratory study to identify costs. *Journal of Education for Business, 84*(5), 283–289.

House, E. R. (2011). Conflict of interest and Campbellian validity. In H. T. Chen, S. I. Donaldson, & M. M. Mark (Eds.), *New Directions for Evaluation: No. 130. Advancing validity in outcome evaluation: Theory and practice* (pp. 69–80). San Francisco, CA: Jossey-Bass.

Huse, I., & McDavid, J. C. (2006). *Literature review: Professionalization of evaluators.* Prepared for the CES Evaluation Professionalization Project, University of Victoria, Victoria, British Columbia.

Jacob, S., & Boisvert, Y. (2010). To be or not to be a profession: Pros, cons and challenges for evaluation. *Evaluation, 16*(4), 349–369.

Jones, S. C., & Worthen, B. R. (1999). AEA members' opinions concerning certification. *American Journal of Evaluation, 20*(3), 495–506.

Julian, S. D., & Ofori-Dankwa, J. C. (2006). Is accreditation good for the strategic decision making of traditional business schools? *Academy of Management Learning & Education, 5*(2), 225–233.

Kilpatrick, J., Dean, K. L., & Kilpatrick, P. (2008). Philosophical concerns about inter-preting AACSB assurance of learning standards. *Journal of Management Inquiry, 17*(3), 200–212.

King, J. A., & Podems, D. (2014). Introduction to professionalizing evaluation: A global perspective on evaluator competencies. *Canadian Journal of Program Evaluation, 28*(3), vii–xv.

Kuchinke, K. P. (2003). Comparing national systems of human resource development: Role and function of post-baccalaureate HRD courses of study in the U.K. and U.S. *Human Resource Development International, 6*(3), 285–299.

Kuchinke, K. P. (2007). Birds of a feather? The critique of the North American business school and its implications for educating HRD practitioners. *Human Resource Development Review, 6*(2), 111–126.

LaVelle, J. M., & Donaldson, S. I. (2010). University-based evaluation training programs in the United States 1980–2008: An empirical examination. *American Journal of Evaluation, 31*(1), 9–23.

Lowrie, A., & Willmott, H. (2009). Accreditation sickness in the consumption of business education: The vacuum in AACSB standard setting. *Management Learning, 40*(4), 411–420.

McDavid, J. C., & Devine, H. A. (2009). *Consortium of Universities for Evaluation Education (CUEE) project: Research on evaluation education at the graduate level in Canadian universities, final report.* Consortium of Universities for Evaluation Education. Retrieved from http://www.evaluationeducation.ca/documents/evaluation%20education%20canada.pdf

McDavid, J. C., & Huse, I. (2006). Will evaluation prosper in the future? *Canadian Journal of Program Evaluation, 21*(3), 47–72.

McKee, M. C., Mills, A. J., & Weatherbee, T. (2005). Institutional field of dreams: Exploring the AACSB and the new legitimacy of Canadian business schools. *Canadian Journal of Administrative Sciences/Revue Canadienne des Sciences de l'Administration, 22*(4), 288–301.

Meyer, J. W., & Rowan, B. (1977). Institutionalized organizations: Formal structure as myth and ceremony. *American Journal of Sociology, 83*(2), 340–363.

NASPAA Standards. (2009). *Commission on Peer Review and Accreditation: National Association of Schools of Public Affairs and Administration Accreditation Standards.* Retrieved from http://naspaaaccreditation.files.wordpress.com/2014/09/naspaa-standards.pdf

Navarro, P. (2008). The MBA core curricula of top-ranked U.S. business schools: A study in failure? *Academy of Management Learning & Education, 7*(1), 108–123.

Nigsch, S., & Schenker-Wicki, A. (2013). Shaping performance: Do international accreditations and quality management really help? *Journal of Higher Education Policy and Management, 35*(6), 668–681.

Patton, M. Q. (2008). *Utilization focused evaluation* (4th ed.). Thousand Oaks, CA: Sage.

Pfeffer, J., & Fong, C. T. (2002). The end of business schools? Less success than meets the eye. *Academy of Management Learning & Education, 1*(1), 78–95.

Podems, D. (2014). Evaluator competencies and professionalizing the field: Where are we now? *Canadian Journal of Program Evaluation, 28*(3), 127–136.

Roller, R. H., Andrews, B. K., & Bovee, S. L. (2003). Specialized accreditation of business schools: A comparison of alternative costs, benefits, and motivations. *Journal of Education for Business, 78*(4), 197–204.

Romero, E. J. (2008). AACSB accreditation: Addressing faculty concerns. *Academy of Management Learning and Education, 7*(2), 245–255.

Rowe, A. (2014). A good start, but we can do better. *Canadian Journal of Program Evaluation, 28*(3), 121–126.

Stepanovich, P., Mueller, J., & Benson, D. (2014). AACSB accreditation and possible unintended consequences: A Deming view. *Journal of Education for Business, 89*(2), 103–109.

Stewart, J., & Sambrook, S. (2012). The historical development of human resource development in the United Kingdom. *Human Resource Development Review, 11*(4), 443–462.

Thomas, L., Billsberry, J., Ambrosini, V., & Barton, H. (2014). Convergence and divergence dynamics in British and French business schools: How will the pressure for accreditation influence these dynamics? *British Journal of Management, 25*(2), 305–319.

Trapnell, J. E. (2007). AACSB International accreditation: The value proposition and a look to the future. *Journal of Management Development, 26*(1), 67–72.

Trapnell, J. E., & Williams, J. R. (2012). AACSB International: An update and perspective. *Issues in Accounting Education, 27*(4), 1071–1076.

Trochim, W. & Riggin, L. (1996, November). *AEA accreditation report.* Unpublished manuscript. American Evaluation Association.

Van Wyhe, G. (2007a). A history of US higher education in accounting, Part I: Situating accounting within the academy. *Issues in Accounting Education, 22*(2), 165–182.

Van Wyhe, G. (2007b). A history of US higher education in accounting, Part II: Reforming accounting within the academy. *Issues in Accounting Education, 22*(3), 481–501.

Whittenburg, G. E., Toole, H., Sciglimpaglia, D., & Medlin, C. (2006). AACSB International accreditation: An Australian perspective. *The Journal of Academic Administration in Higher Education, 2*(1–2), 9–13.

Worthen, B. R. (1999). Critical challenges confronting certification of evaluators. *American Journal of Evaluation, 20*(3), 533–555.

Yunker, J. A. (2000). Viewpoint: Doing things the hard way—Problems with mission-linked AACSB accreditation standards and suggestions for improvement. *Journal of Education for Business, 75*(6), 348–353.

Zachmeier, A., Cho, Y., & Kim, M. (2014). The same but different: HRD master's programmes in the United States. *Human Resource Development International, 17*(3), 318–338.

Zammuto, R. (2008). Accreditation and globalization of business. *Academy of Management Learning and Education, 7*(2), 256–268.

JAMES C. MCDAVID is a professor in the School of Public Administration at the University of Victoria, British Columbia.

IRENE HUSE is a PhD candidate in the School of Public Administration at the University of Victoria, British Columbia.

5

Credentialed Evaluator Designation Program, the Canadian Experience

Keiko Kuji-Shikatani

Abstract

The Credentialed Evaluator (CE) designation is a service provided by Canadian Evaluation Society (CES) to its members, who may elect to become credentialed on a voluntary basis. The designation means that the holder has provided evidence of the education and experience required by the CES to be a competent evaluator. The author briefly examines the impetus for the CE designation, the value it represents for the Canadian evaluation community, the development of the system including structure and administration, and how it is evolving as we learn from professionalizing evaluation in Canada. Concerns expressed during the development of the Competencies for Canadian Evaluation Practice mirrored those expressed about the development of a professional designation. The CE designation is about providing a path for new evaluators and a clearer direction for more established evaluators for their ongoing development. © Wiley Periodicals, Inc., and the American Evaluation Association.

I n May 2010, the Canadian Evaluation Society (CES) launched the CES Credentialed Evaluator (CE) designation designed to define, recognize, and promote the practice of ethical, high-quality, and competent evaluation in Canada. The CE designation is a service provided by CES to its members, who elect to become credentialed on a voluntary basis. The designation means that the holder provided evidence of the education and experience required by the CES to be a competent evaluator. It allows CEs to be recognized for what they have achieved and for their ongoing commitment to learning and improving their practice as program evaluators. The impetus for the CE designation, its value for the Canadian evaluation community, the development of the structure and administration of the program, and how it is evolving are described in this chapter.

Practice-Based Membership

CES represents the evaluation community in Canada, which is seen (Borys, Gauthier, Kishchuk, & Roy, 2005) as a "practice-based membership" of roughly 1,800 individuals in 11 regionally based chapters that include internal evaluators, external evaluators, and academia. Evaluation is currently a $67.4 million dollar business in the Canadian federal government, involving some 497 internal human resources and additional external (consulting) resources used in the large majority (73%) of federal government evaluations (MacDonald & Buchanan, 2011). The Canadian federal government as a major consumer and producer of evaluations in Canada has a noticeable influence on the Canadian evaluation community (Buchanan & Kuji-Shikatani, 2014). Roughly 30% of the CES members are employed by the federal government and 19% by provincial governments as internal evaluators conducting and managing evaluations. Another 20% of the CES members are external evaluators in the private sector primarily in consulting firms undertaking evaluations for the public, not-for-profit, and private sectors. Regional distribution of the CES membership is influenced by the strong presence of the federal government in central Canada, with 30% of CES members located in the National Capital Region (Ottawa) and another 20% in Ontario. The Canadian evaluation community and the CES have matured with the federal government evaluation function. Fewer than 10% of the CES members are academics, a distinct differentiation from the American Evaluation Association (AEA), where about 40% are employed in colleges and universities (MacDonald & Buchanan, 2011). The proportion of academics in CES membership is small when compared to AEA internal but evaluators in government work collaboratively with external evaluators from both *academia* and *private firms*.

Laying the Foundations to Become a Profession

CES has pursued several key initiatives over the past 35 years that help to build a strong foundation and identity for the Canadian evaluation community in regard to what constitutes ethical, quality evaluation practice. CES Guidelines for Ethical Conduct that address issues of competence, integrity, and accountability for evaluators was developed through extensive consultations with members from 1988 until approved in 1996, reviewed and reaffirmed by National Council in 2006 and 2008 (Canadian Evaluation Society, 2008a). CES's flagship training course, the Essential Skills

NEW DIRECTIONS FOR EVALUATION • DOI: 10.1002/ev

Series (ESS), was designed in 1999 to enhance program evaluation skills and promote the professional evaluation practice across Canada. ESS (four one-day modules—Understanding Program Evaluation, Building an Evaluation Framework, Improving Program Performance, and Evaluating for Results) has been updated over the years to accommodate the evolution of the evaluation field. The audiences are new evaluators who manage evaluation projects for their organizations and those wanting a refresher course on the main program evaluation concepts and issues (Canadian Evaluation Society, 1999).

CES commissioned a study in 2002, commonly referred to as the Core Body of Knowledge (CBK) study, *The Canadian Evaluation Society Project in Support of Advocacy and Professional Development: Evaluation Benefits, Outputs, and Knowledge Elements*, to gain a better understanding of the evaluation practice knowledge base. The CBK identified 151 knowledge, skill, and practice items within six categories: ethics (integrity and competence), evaluation planning and design, data collection, data analysis and interpretation, communication and interpersonal skills, and project management associated with evaluation practice (Zorzi, McGuire, & Perrin, 2002). In 2008 (again in 2012), CES formally adopted the Program Evaluation Standards as a longstanding, active member of the Joint Committee on Standards for Educational Evaluation in discussing what constitutes quality practice in evaluation.

Canadian Debate on Professionalizing Evaluation Practice

The ongoing debate on "professionalizing" evaluation practice in Canada, specifically through a professional designation, certification, and/or accreditation, was fueled by:

- issues of poor evaluation quality, underfunding, and questions on usefulness leading to credibility problems (Gussman, 2005);
- lack of clear demarcations and defined parameters for the evaluation function, as well as standardized entrance requirements (notably in comparison to the audit community), was seen to be a challenge (Canadian Evaluation Society, 2006); and
- the questioning by evaluators of their professional identity, speaking of a desire to better define the nature of their work, and examining means to recognize the skills and knowledge required to do that work (Borys et al., 2005).

In response, the CES commissioned a 2006 study through a request for proposals (RFP) seeking an action plan that would aid the CES in establishing a professional designation system. A consortium of experienced evaluators responded to the RFP and produced a comprehensive *Action Plan for the Canadian Evaluation Society with Respect to Professional Standards for*

Evaluators. The report urged the CES to move forward with a program of professional designations and suggested that core competencies were fundamental to doing so (Canadian Evaluation Society, 2007a). The CES responded to the report (Canadian Evaluation Society, 2007c), supporting the development of a credential level of designation as a first step in exploring this approach to professionalization. The issue was put to the CES membership through an extensive consultation process in 2007 consisting of four mechanisms:

- an interactive public exchange on the CES web forum EDÉ-L;
- private e-mails received by the Chair of the Member Services Committee of National Council;
- CES chapter events and briefs received due to a call for input from various organizations with an interest in the professional designations of evaluators (Cousins, Maicher, & Malik, 2007); and
- a presentation of consultation results at a town hall meeting convened at the 2007 CES Conference, including an open mike discussion on the issue.

Although there were (and are) mixed feelings on the pursuit of any type of professional designation, CES decided in August 2007 to move forward with a CE designation (Canadian Evaluation Society, 2007b). Five fundamental principles guiding the effort were inclusiveness, partnering, utility, feasibility, and transparency (Canadian Evaluation Society-National Council, 2007).

Critical elements of the CE designation are ethics, standards, and competencies—all of which were addressed in the development of the CES Professional Designations Program (PDP; Canadian Evaluation Society, 2010b). The CES National Council noted that a well-structured and agreed upon knowledge base is essential to any system of professional designation and proposed a crosswalk (cross-referencing to determine points of overlap and difference) of existing knowledge bases that support a comprehensive list of evaluator competencies. Competencies are the knowledge, skills, and dispositions program evaluators need to achieve standards of practice for sound evaluations (Stevahn, King, Ghere, & Minnema, 2005). CES Professional Designations Core Committee conducted that crosswalk building on the work of Establishing Essential Competencies for Program Evaluators (Stevahn et al., 2005). Key sources were:

- 2002 version of Treasury Board Secretariat Competencies for Evaluators in the Government of Canada (as a major employer and purchaser of evaluation);
- 2007 CES Essential Skills Series;
- 2002 Core Body of Knowledge (Zorzi et al., 2002);

- the 2004 Joint Committee Program Evaluation Standards (adopted by CES National Council);
- the 2004 version of the American Evaluation Association's Guidelines; and
- the United Nations Competencies for Evaluators in the United Nations System—to provide a broader international perspective (Canadian Evaluation Society, 2008b).

The crosswalk informed the development of the CES Competencies for Canadian Evaluation Practice by examining materials from organizations that primarily function to advance the professional practice of program evaluation (Canadian Evaluation Society, 2008a). After membership consultations, town hall meetings across Canada, and work with experts, the Competencies for Canadian Evaluation Practice were placed into five competency domains (Table 5.1) with specific competencies under each. The categories are essential components of overall evaluation practice, comprehensive without being exhaustive, and include the increasing work done in the area of performance measurement in Canada.

Competencies for Canadian Evaluation Practice, along with ethics and standards, are the foundation for the CE designation program and provide direction for the evaluation community (Canadian Evaluation Society, 2010a) as follows:

- informs evaluation practitioners about the knowledge and skills required to be competent and guide their professional development;
- alerts learning organizations and service providers to the type of education and professional development required to support the discipline;
- specifies for firms/organizations the expertise to incorporate in job descriptions or seek in contracting evaluation services; and
- helps program managers working with evaluation professionals in terms of the expertise they can expect to receive.

Concerns expressed during the development of the Competencies mirrored those expressed about the development of a professional designation such as barriers to entry, the immaturity of the Canadian evaluation education system and private sector training providers to support evaluation competency development, and the richness brought to the community through diverse educational and experiential paradigms. Other concerns were about the potential for negative effects if evaluation practice was overly uniform in its defined knowledge and skills base. Worries about generic evaluation skills (versus subject matter expertise) were frequently raised. Extensive consultations and use of experts went a long way toward addressing member issues (Buchanan & Kuji-Shikatani, 2014; Borys et al., 2005).

Table 5.1. Competencies for Canadian Evaluation Practice

1.0   Reflective Practice competencies focus on the fundamental norms and values underlying evaluation practice and awareness of one's evaluation expertise and needs for growth.

1.1   Applies professional evaluation standards
1.2   Acts ethically and strives for integrity and honesty
1.3   Respects all stakeholders
1.4   Considers human rights and the public welfare in evaluation practice
1.5   Provides independent and impartial perspective
1.6   Aware of self as an evaluator (knowledge, skills, and dispositions) and reflects on personal evaluation practice (competencies and areas for growth)
1.7   Pursues professional networks and self-development to enhance evaluation practice

2.0   Technical Practice competencies focus on the specialized aspects of evaluation, such as design, data collection, analysis, interpretation, and reporting.

2.1   Understands the knowledge base of evaluation (theories, models, types, methods, and tools)
2.2   Specifies program theory
2.3   Determines the purpose for the evaluation
2.4   Determines program evaluability
2.5   Frames evaluation questions
2.6   Develops evaluation designs
2.7   Defines evaluation methods (quantitative, qualitative, or mixed)
2.8   Identifies data sources
2.9   Develops reliable and valid measures/tools
2.10 Collects data
2.11 Assesses validity of data
2.12 Assesses reliability of data
2.13 Assesses trustworthiness of data
2.14 Analyzes and interprets data
2.15 Draws conclusions and makes recommendations
2.16 Reports evaluation findings and results

3.0   Situational Practice competencies focus on the application of evaluative thinking in analyzing and attending to the unique interests, issues, and contextual circumstances in which evaluation skills are being applied.

3.1   Respects the uniqueness of the site
3.2   Examines organizational, political, community, and social contexts
3.3   Identifies impacted stakeholders
3.4   Identifies the interests of all stakeholders
3.5   Serves the information needs of intended users
3.6   Attends to issues of evaluation use
3.7   Attends to issues of organizational and environmental change
3.8   Applies evaluation competencies to organization and program measurement challenges
3.9   Shares evaluation expertise

4.0   Management Practice competencies focus on the process of managing a project/evaluation, such as budgeting, coordinating resources, and supervising.

4.1   Defines work parameters, plans, and agreements
4.2   Attends to issues of evaluation feasibility
4.3   Identifies required resources (human, financial, and physical)

(Continued)

Table 5.1. Continued

4.4   Monitors resources (human, financial, and physical)
4.5   Coordinates and supervises others
4.6   Reports on progress and results
4.7   Identifies and mitigates problems/issues
5.0   Interpersonal Practice competencies focus on people skills, such as
      communication, negotiation, conflict resolution, collaboration, and diversity.
5.1   Uses written communication skills and technologies
5.2   Uses verbal communication skills
5.3   Uses listening skills
5.4   Uses negotiation skills
5.5   Uses conflict resolution skills
5.6   Uses facilitation skills (group work)
5.7   Uses interpersonal skills (individual and teams)
5.8   Uses collaboration/partnering skills
5.9   Attends to issues of diversity and culture
5.10   Demonstrates professional credibility

Competencies-Based Professional Designations Program

In order to qualify, a CE applicant is required to provide:

- evidence of graduate-level degree or certificate related to evaluation;
- evidence of two years (full-time equivalent) evaluation-related work experience within the last 10 years; and
- indicators of education and/or experience related to 70% of the competencies in *each* of the five domains of Competencies (Canadian Evaluation Society, 2010b).

Criteria for the designation were collaboratively defined through numerous member interactions based on information about CES membership such as the *Survey of Evaluation Practice and Issues in Canada* (Borys et al., 2005), which found that, among the producers of evaluation ($N = 638$), a completed master's degree is the norm (61%), and there are as many PhDs (16%) as there are evaluators with bachelor's degree. The Ontario Qualifications Framework (Ontario Ministry of Training, Colleges and Universities, 2009), which describes the main purposes and features and outlines the knowledge and skills expected of holders of the master's and post-bachelor's degree certificate programs, showed alignment with the competencies listed in the Competencies. These ensured confidence as to the appropriateness of the education requirement. However, since evaluators come from a broad range of disciplines (Borys et al., 2005) and few graduate certificates in program evaluation existed or were in planning stages, the field of study was left undefined.

Grand parenting—related to the education qualification only—is available to CES members who were part of CES as of June 1, 2009. Initially, grand parenting was to be for a limited time to recognize long-time CES members who began their practice before having a graduate-level education became the standard. After that initial period, the CES National Council decided to keep grand parenting, along with the other inclusive practices recognizing the evaluation diversity, available on a permanent basis. Foreign-educated CES members may have their education qualifications assessed by external organizations and submit the assessment of equivalency. Also, Prior Learning Assessment and Recognition is available for a separate assessment fee to address those experienced evaluators who may be able to demonstrate the equivalent of that education through extensive work experience and professional development.

For professional experience, applicants are asked to provide evidence of two years (full-time equivalent) related effort within the last 10 years. Statements documenting what they have done regarding employment, practicum, volunteer, and other evaluation endeavors are submitted. Note that one of the common questions asked in the information sessions was whether teaching evaluation qualifies as evaluation-related work experience.

For supporting documents, applicants provide letters of reference using the Credentialed Evaluator Application Sponsor Form (Canadian Evaluation Society, 2010c). The requirement for at least two-year full-time equivalent work experience within the past 10 years was based on consultations across the country and from references such as the *Survey of Evaluation Practice and Issues in Canada* (Borys et al., 2005). The 10-year window recognizes the wide variations in the availability of evaluation-related work throughout Canada, especially in nonurban areas. Some Canadian practitioners reported evaluation as an important but not major component of their work, primarily due to insufficient demand.

To demonstrate their Competencies for Canadian Evaluation Practice, applicants draw selectively from their education and/or experience and align this to at least 70% of the five competency domains. The alignment is explained in a brief narrative with a maximum of 1,000 characters permitted in the application form for each competency. This requirement is a reflective process, with the narrative demonstrating to reviewers that the applicant understands and has the skill and knowledge dimensions in the competency. The Competencies for Canadian Evaluation Practice are supplemented with descriptors, providing greater definition for each competency to aid in this process. While applicants need not have experience and formal education directly related to a competency, they must show that collectively they have the required competence (Canadian Evaluation Society, 2010c). This third qualification (in addition to skill and content knowledge) necessitates that the applicant is asked to use their educational and professional experience to provide evidence of competency. Within each domain, expertise must be shown for a minimum of 70% of the competencies listed but did not define which are essential or more important than others.

Figure 5.1. Flowchart of CE Application Process

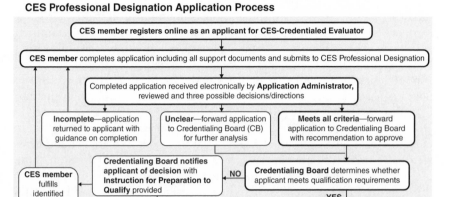

This accommodates the diversity in Canadian evaluation practice as well as Canadians' valuing of diversity and inclusion.

Administration of the Professional Designations Program

CES manages the CE designation within their PDP under a vice president responsible for same. Applications are submitted online through the CES-CE secure website handled by a PDP application administrator. The nonrefundable fee is $485 and is for application processing within a three-year time frame (renewable upon repayment) and making the decision. (For applicants needing to provide qualifications under PLAR, a fee of $550 is charged since this necessitates a separate review process with a level of customization for each application.) CE designation applicants may take up to 36 months to complete their application. Applications may be submitted in either English or French, Canada's two official languages, and be reviewed in the language of the application. (See Figure 5.1, flowchart of CE application process.)

The CES PDP is a major service for CES members with different components of the program embedded in existing National Council areas such as administration, membership, and professional learning. Also, new structures, resources, and processes were put in place to support this service.

CES Credentialing Board

The three qualification requirements, along with evidence of maintaining the designation (40 hours of ongoing learning and professional development every three years; Canadian Evaluation Society, 2013), once submitted are reviewed by the CES Credentialing Board, which is the decision-making body for the PDP. It considers the merits of a member's application for becoming officially credentialed as an evaluation professional by the CES. The Board consists of members who are experts from the Canadian evaluation field and are recognized as the CES Fellows and National Award winners.

Decisions regarding designations and maintenance of the CE status are made by the Board using the CES-CE secure website. An application is reviewed by two Board members and by a third member if the decision of the first two is not the same. The decision is communicated to the applicant through the CES President. When the CE designation is awarded, the CES member's name is added to the CES-maintained, publicly available, registry of CE on the CES website. Appeals can be registered within 30 days of notification of a "further preparation needed" decision. Appellants are encouraged to review and augment their application for the appeal as the shortfall may be a matter of inadequate description of competencies. Appealed decisions undergo a further review process with two new reviewers and a third member review if the decision by the first two reviewers is not the same.

The designation is about providing a path for new evaluators and a clearer direction for more established ones for their ongoing development. If the application is incomplete or if they require additional education or experience, the applicant is provided with advice on how to meet the qualifications including further learning needs as part of any deferred application. Applicants requiring further learning do not pay the application fee as long as they are within the 36 months period of the initial fee payment.

Professional Learning Requirements for Credentialed Evaluators

After the initial costs for the PDP are paid, the PDP is set up to be basically cost neutral. PDP has only an additional annual CES membership fee of $50 from CEs to record and have their 40 hours of professional learning over three years reviewed. Some employers, mainly in the private sector as well as some in the public sector, have offered financial support to help defray some of the expense associated with the CE application and maintenance. Each CE is assigned an account within the CES-CE system to input courses and development at any time. Accounts are accessed by the application administrator at the three-year mark. If CEs don't have the requisite 40 hours of development activities, they are contacted in regard to maintaining their designated status (Canadian Evaluation Society, 2014).

NEW DIRECTIONS FOR EVALUATION • DOI: 10.1002/ev

Challenges, Collaborations, Continuum—*Learning as We Go*

When the CE designation program was launched, approximately 10% of the CES members signed up to create their application accounts; however, they were slow to actually submit their applications. After a year from the launch at the CES 2011 National Conference in Edmonton during the first face-to-face meeting, the Credentialing Board discussed the low rates of application. Two factors seemed relevant. First, demand as in those commissioning evaluations seeing the designation as a quality measure and using it in the choice of evaluators, those employed in evaluation positions, and those engaged in contract assignments.

Secondly there is supply. The CES anticipates that the rate of application will accelerate, especially by senior practitioners in government, nonprofit, and private sectors.

The Credentialing Board suggested that CES create a one-year temporary "fast-track" application for the CES designation of CE as an approach to bringing in those who are at and well beyond the CE level of experience (Canadian Evaluation Society, 2011).The idea was brought to the National Council, and informal consultations with CES members took place during the conference. The Council met at the 2011 National Conference and discussed a number of concerns including:

- The current competency-based application seems unattractive for senior practitioners and may be constraining application submissions from a significant number of very experienced and long-term CES evaluation practitioners.
- A critical mass of CEs is important as more individuals begin using the designation and the Competencies for Canadian Evaluation Practice as part of their business practice. Doing so will spur demand for the credential in both internal and external evaluation practice in the country.
- Once experienced, senior evaluators have applied for/acquired the CE, future applications would be from CES members that were envisioned to apply—those with a graduate-level education, two years of professional experience in evaluation, and culminating in a minimum of 70% of the CES competencies.

Following the deliberations, a decision was reached to invite experienced evaluators from the CES membership to apply for the CE designation through an expedited application process. The fast track was temporarily available for only one year with invitations sent to CES members who have:

- been a CES member for seven years;
- graduate-level education; and
- declared evaluation as a primary or major part of their work.

NEW DIRECTIONS FOR EVALUATION • DOI: 10.1002/ev

CES members received e-mail invitations as well as communication through a website that these criteria were used as a proxy for "experienced evaluator" and may not fully capture all those who may wish to use the expedited application process. A streamlined or fast-track process has been employed in other professional associations for similar new programs. It was positioned as a means to honor long-term CES members and recognize their extensive experience and expertise. The invitations were not meant to be exclusionary and other experienced CES members who wanted to apply through this method were invited to write to the vice president of the PDP to express their interest (Canadian Evaluation Society, 2011). A number of CES members contacted CES to be considered for the fast-track process. The Professional Designations Program Committee on the National Council reviewed these requests, and decisions were communicated to the applicants based on the merit of the claims.

An additional application and review process was set up on the CES PDP website in coordination with the National Council under the management of the vice president as the application administrator and the web developer. This streamlining was designed to not negatively impact the decision process for awarding the CE designation. Fast-track applications were reviewed by the Credentialing Board, applying the same criteria (graduate-level education, two years of professional experience in evaluation, and 70% of CES competencies) for awarding the designation. The Credentialing Board requested additional information if required. Decisions were made to award the designation based on the fast-track application or to recommend that the applicant go through the regular application process with suggestions (without an additional fee).

Some Lessons Learned

From the CES PDP website data, 256 CEs representing about 14% of CES members have chosen to voluntarily apply and were awarded the professional designation. In addition to observations and issues brought up previously, we have learned about the designation system through the results of a 2014 survey of CES members conducted by Gauthier, Kishchuk, Borys, and Roy in 2014. These data described the characteristics of those who have and have not applied for the CE designation and assessed some features of the system.

A first lesson learned is in relation to the time it takes to initiate the system. One inference from survey results was the conclusion that its authors thought that it was off to a good start in Canada. Keeping in mind that some CES members might not be full practicing evaluators or are more administrators, the total base of those who sought professional designation might be lower than assumed, and thus the percentage of designated evaluators might be closer to 30% (Gauthier, 2014). Additionally, there is no standard to compare those early pursuers of such credentials in similar evaluation organizations, and it is possible and suspected that activities like these start slowly. This perception will be useful to others considering such a system as they *factor in an elongated start-up period of time until a tipping point is reached.*

A second lesson comes from what the survey found out about credentialed evaluators. They are composed of senior CES members who are:

- likely to work in the private sector (52% vs. 19% of non-CEs),
- experienced (69% with 11+ years vs. 29% of non-CEs, older—56% are 50+ vs. 32% of non-CEs, higher income—47% make $100+k vs. 20% of non-CEs),
- more engaged with CES (longer term members—44% for 11+ years vs. 10% of non-CEs, more who have volunteered for CES—67% vs. 22% of non-CEs), and
- likely to hold another designation (30% vs. 22% of non-CEs).

The investigators noted that CES members new to the evaluation community see the designation as a professional career goal. So it is essential to *keep learning* more about the state of the designation through (a) membership surveys such as the one just described and (b) by examination and evaluation by the evaluation community both in Canada and internationally. The latter could be done via logic models of the structure of the system (Canadian Evaluation Society, 2010b).

Moreover, what was learned from the survey supported the grand parenting and fast-tracking paths taken by CES. These paths were well received by respondents who qualified for using them. It was informative to learn what new evaluators were thinking about the option of pursuing the status.

Together, these two outcomes point toward the critical need for organizations following routes like these to fully understand the nature of their overall group membership and subpopulations within it. Sensitivity in undertaking ventures like accreditation, certification, credentialing, or combinations of them must take into account where subsets of the total population are in their thinking and perceptions. Not doing so could lead to acrimony and at worst failure.

A third lesson is that the enhanced program brought attention to the competencies and professionalization of evaluation. CES members who have applied or are applying for designation are reviewing and thinking deeply about the Competencies as part of the requirements to qualify. Beyond that, CEs must participate in ongoing professional development and learning to retain the status based on the Competencies for Canadian Evaluation Practice that is growing steadily (Canadian Evaluation Society, 2014). Along the same lines, Credentialing Board members who are reviewing submissions to qualify for the designation are also increasing our understanding of competencies. Similarly, members of the Canadian Consortium of Universities for Evaluation Education (Kuji-Shikatani, McDavid, Cousins, & Buchanan, 2013) and providers of professional evaluation education programs in Canada and internationally (Certificate of Advanced Study in Evaluation at Claremont Graduate University, http://www.cgu.edu/pages/670.asp) are using the Competencies for Canadian Evaluation Practice to develop their programs. Finally, more employers and organizations who commission evaluations are using the Competencies jobs and contract requirements (Buchanan & Kuji-Shikatani, 2014). Those who commission evaluations are gaining experience with working with CEs and are now including *Credentialed Evaluator* as an asset in their RFP or in job descriptions.

The CE designation and the Competencies for Canadian Evaluation Practice that the designation is based on are admittedly in their infancy and need to be revisited regularly as our profession evolves. For example, responding to the international request to share the Canadian experience of professionalization of evaluation, the Canadian Journal of Program Evaluation is preparing a special edition for 2015 in the International Year of Evaluation focused on the CE designation experience. CES will continue to learn and share our experience in enhancing the professionalization of evaluation and its contribution to the betterment of society through collaborative efforts.

References

Borys, S., Gauthier, B., Kishchuk, N., & Roy, S. (2005, November). *Survey of evaluation practice and issues in Canada.* Paper presented at the Joint 2005 CES/AEA Conference, Toronto, Canada.

Buchanan, H., & Kuji-Shikatani, K. (2014). Evaluator competencies: The Canadian experience. *The Canadian Journal of Program Evaluation, 28*(3), 29–47.

Canadian Evaluation Society. (1999). *Specialized training.* Retrieved from Canadian Evaluation Society website: http://www.evaluationcanada.ca/site.cgi?s=3&ss=3&_lang=en

Canadian Evaluation Society. (2006, May). *Request for proposals for fact finding regarding evaluator credentialing.*

Canadian Evaluation Society. (2007a, January). *An action plan for the CES with respect to Professional Standards for Evaluators.*

Canadian Evaluation Society. (2007b, March). *Response to proposed action plan for the CES respect to Professional Standards for Evaluators.*

Canadian Evaluation Society. (2007c, November). *Professional Designations Project Plan.*

Canadian Evaluation Society. (2008a). *CES Guidelines for Ethical Conduct.* Retrieved from http://www.evaluationcanada.ca/site.cgi?s=5&ss=4&_lang=EN

Canadian Evaluation Society. (2008b). *Crosswalk of evaluator competencies,* Version 10. Retrieved from http://evaluationcanada.ca/distribution/20080312_ces_professional_designation_core_committee.pdf

Canadian Evaluation Society. (2010a, April). *Competencies for Canadian Evaluation Practice.* Retrieved from http://www.evaluationcanada.ca/txt/2_competencies_cdn_evaluation_practice.pdf

Canadian Evaluation Society. (2010b, April). *Professional Designations Program Archives.* Retreived from http://www.evaluationcanada.ca/professional-designations-project-archives

Canadian Evaluation Society. (2010c, November). *Professional Designations Program Applications Guide*. Retreived from http://www.evaluationcanada.ca/txt/5_pdp_applicant_guide.pdf

Canadian Evaluation Society. (October, 2011). *CES members invited to fast tracked application for CE designation*. Retrieved from http://www.evaluationcanada.ca/site.cgi?s=1&ss=1&_lang=en&num=01397

Canadian Evaluation Society. (2014). *Learning activities for credentialed evaluator renewal*. Retrieved from http://www.evaluationcanada.ca/credentialed-evaluators

Canadian Evaluation Society-National Council. (2007, November 22). *Professional Designations Project work in progress*. Retreived from http://old.evaluationcanada.ca/txt/cespd_20081117_e.pdf

Cousins, J., Maicher, B., & Malik, S. (2007). *Integration of consultative input: Professional designations for evaluators*. Ottawa, Canada: Canadian Evaluation Society.

Gauthier, B., Kishchuk, N., Borys, S., & Roy, S. N. (2014, June 16). *The CES Professional Designations Program: Views from CES members*. Paper presented at the CES Conference, Ottawa, Canada.

Gussman, T. (2005). *Improving the professionalization of evaluation*. Prepared for the Centre of Excellence in Evaluation. Ottawa, Canada: Treasury Board of Canada Secretariat.

Kuji-Shikatani, K., McDavid, J., Cousins, J. B., & Buchanan, H. (2013). Consortium of universities for evaluation education and its impact on professionalizing evaluation in Canada. *Japanese Journal of Evaluation Studies*, 12(2), 11–22.

MacDonald, W., & Buchanan, H. (2011). *Evaluation ethics*. Paper presented at the annual meeting of the American Evaluation Association, Washington, DC.

Ontario Ministry of Training, Colleges and Universities. (2009). *The ontario qualifications framework*. Toronto, Canada: Government of Ontario.

Stevahn, L., King, J. A., Ghere, G., & Minnema, J. (2005). Establishing essential competencies for program evaluators. *American Journal of Evaluation*, 26(1), 43–59.

Zorzi, R., McGuire, M., & Perrin, B. (2002). *Canadian Evaluation Society Project in support of advocacy and professional development*. Retrieved from Canadian Evaluation Society website: http://consultation.evaluationcanada.ca/results.htm

KEIKO KUJI-SHIKATANI *(Credentialed Evaluator) is an education officer, Research, Evaluation and Capacity Building Branch, Student Achievement Division at the Ontario Ministry of Education.*

6

Evaluator Certification and Credentialing Revisited: A Survey of American Evaluation Association Members in the United States

Michelle Baron Seidling

Abstract

Conversations over the past few years have included issues of evaluator skills and experience that are vital to the field of evaluation. Many professions administer certification or credentialing programs to ensure quality work, enhance professionalism in the field, and increase marketability for its members. Is the evaluation field ready for such an endeavor? In this chapter are the results of a survey of American Evaluation Association members within the United States regarding the feasibility, need, and potential for certification or credentialing in the future. © Wiley Periodicals, Inc., and the American Evaluation Association.

T he dawn of the 21st century brought with it a discussion regarding *certification*—"the formal process used to determine individuals' relative levels of competence (knowledge and skill) in evaluation and, for those who reach or exceed specified minimal levels, to issue certificates attesting that the individual is competent to do good evaluation work" (Worthen, 1999, p. 535) and *credentialing*—"the process whereby individuals who complete a specified set of evaluation courses and/or field experiences are issued a credential attesting to this fact, with the presumption that completion of the required evaluation courses or experiences prepares those individuals to perform competently as evaluators" (p. 535).

Inherent in certification and credentialing are concerns about the protection of the consumer or user of services, branding of the evaluation field, ethical and procedural standards for it, and evaluator competencies (Altschuld, 1999; Bickman, 1999, Stevahn, King, Ghere, & Minnema, 2005). A 1998 survey of American Evaluation Association (AEA) members in the United States (Jones & Worthen, 1999) showed mixed views on the potential for certification and credentialing programs for evaluators.

Some of the challenges or barriers to efforts about these topics have been addressed by other chapters in this issue, but numerous ones remain such as depth and maintenance of competence, credentialing versus certification, and the interdisciplinary nature of evaluation. Evaluator status, certification use and value, and leadership are important to the field for a myriad of reasons, including credibility, legitimacy, and branding.

Certification and credentialing have reentered the conversation via the AEA Thought Leader Discussion Series (King, 2012), commentary from members of the Canadian Evaluation Society, the think tank session on evaluator certification presented at the 2012 AEA annual conference (Altschuld et al., 2012), and discussions on EVALTALK and social media sources. Further, these topics have also been center stage at the last two annual AEA conferences. The theme two years ago of "Complex Ecologies" (American Evaluation Association, 2012) emphasized that evaluators have responsibilities for technical and tactical skills in completing an evaluation and for building relationships with stakeholders and other interested parties. Certification could demonstrate what evaluators bring to the table via education and experience and the degree to which those internal and external to the evaluation profession embrace those qualities. The focus of the 2013 conference was the "the State of Evaluation in the 21st Century" (American Evaluation Association, 2013). It covered developments in information gathering, collaboration, and the expanding reach of evaluation on future evaluative relationships. By pursuing certification and/or credentialing, we could show the professionalism and teamwork that is a characteristic of many respected professions. To be meaningful for evaluators and those whom they serve, certification and credentialing must be a collaborative, long-term effort. The title for AEA 2014, "Visionary Evaluation for a Sustainable, Equitable Future," may likewise generate further conversation on these vital topics. Such exchanges would help increase knowledge and awareness about certification/credentialing, understand the benefits and shortcomings thereof, make informed decisions for potential certification/credentialing programs, and propagate professionalism within the evaluation community.

This chapter contains the results and analysis of a survey of evaluators conducted in 2014. This was an exploratory study and was not predicated on the assumption that a certification and/or credentialing process of any kind would be implemented. The instrument was not seeking agreement or disagreement going these routes; rather, its intent was to obtain feedback on the feasibility, need, and potential for certification or credentialing at some point down the road. Participation in the study was voluntary. Answering any specific question was not required, and respondent involvement could be terminated at any time. Topics included competency, governance, and procedures of a potential certification or credentialing program. I hope that the information gained will enhance the certification/credentialing debate.

Survey Structure

It is necessary to take into account that while many evaluation organizations offer courses, and workshops on a variety of evaluation topics (e.g., AEA Summer Institute, The Evaluators' Institute, and Claremont Graduate University), and give certificates upon completion, the definitions of certification and credentialing in the context of this study refer to a centralized process that would be across the entire evaluation community. So, prominent in the survey were clear definitions of the terms to avoid confusion on the part of respondents and to have them all on the same page when they shared their perceptions.

The survey development was a collaborative effort of three seasoned evaluators (Seidling and the coeditors of this volume, Altschuld and Engle), all AEA members for many years and well acquainted with the structure, policies, and procedures of the organization. These individuals do not work for or represent AEA, and given its very large membership, the sampling frame was immense and appropriate. After several iterations, the team developed a 16-question survey based on the one done by Jones and Worthen (completed in 1998 and published in 1999), the 2012 Thought Leader Discussion (King, 2012), and the 2012 think tank session (Altschuld, et al., 2012). The authors established face validity of the survey via the thorough review process of questions based on the survey intent, the instrument used in the previous investigation in 1998, and other discussions on certification and credentialing within the evaluation community.

After obtaining approval from the sponsoring Institutional Review Board (Oregon State University) and permission from AEA to send the survey to members in the United States, distribution through Survey Monkey began in the summer of 2014. Analysis and write-up were completed several months later. Descriptive statistics were used for the quantitative responses, and thematic analysis was used to analyze the qualitative responses. There were four questions focusing on certification/credentialing as a whole, three on the governance of a certification/credentialing process, three about the criteria for which evaluators could be judged for the relevant status in the certification/credentialing system, one open-ended item for additional comments, and several about respondent demographics. Fifteen questions were of a quantitative nature (Likert scales, multiple choice items), and one question was qualitative.

The author received from the AEA administrative office a random sample of 1,000 out of the 5,558 AEA members residing in the United States. The initial emailing resulted in nine email messages being returned as undeliverable, 10 going to those who previously opted out from receiving survey correspondence but were still on the AEA email list, and one participant who disagreed with the consent form and did not complete the survey. The final sample consisted of 150 responses out of a total sample of 980 (15.3% response rate). While inferences to the evaluation population as a whole may not be generalized because of the low response rate, this exploratory effort still provides valuable insights into evaluator viewpoints regarding certification and credentialing. Especially pertinent here is the fact that some findings were quite parallel to those of more than 15 years ago, leading to a number of conclusions similar to those of that earlier period. The implications of this overall pattern will be explained later in the chapter.

Results

Table 6.1 contains the respondent demographics for this survey. As expected, evaluators come from a variety of evaluation work settings. The largest areas in sample were 41.18% of evaluators working in university settings, 31.09% are self-employed, 30.25% in nonprofit settings, and 17.65% of evaluators in consulting firms.

The low return rate may be partially attributed to the fact that this survey was administered during the summer, which may have conflicted with personal agendas. Although the original idea was to launch it in the spring, the time needed to obtain IRB and AEA approval was elongated, which led to the survey being distributed much later than planned. The author conducted both the initial survey launch and the follow-up email during the height of the summer, when many individuals have busy family schedules and obligations. Additionally, while the 1998 survey included an extensive follow-up of nonrespondents, the survey authors did not have AEA permission to contact participants beyond a follow-up email message.

Table 6.2 has the results of questions pertaining to the favorability of various aspects of certification and credentialing. An important distinction from the 1998 survey is that this survey specifically asked participants whether they favor certification and credentialing rather than attempting to infer that information from responses that did not directly deal with that point.

Parallel to what Jones and Worthen observed, this current survey also led to mixed results. For example, 38.74% agreed or strongly agreed that a certification system should be implemented, and 46.81% agreed or strongly agreed that a credentialing system should be implemented, which was

Table 6.1. Demographic Characteristics of Respondents

In What Setting(s) Do You Perform Evaluation Work?	
University	41.18%
Self-employed	31.09%
Nonprofit	30.25%
Consulting firm	17.65%
State organization	10.08%
Federal organization	9.24%
School system	9.24%
For-profit business	8.40%
Local organization	7.56%
Not applicable/not currently a practicing evaluator	0.84%
Other[a]	5.88%

What Is Your Highest Academic Degree?	
Doctorate	57.14%
Masters	34.45%
Bachelors	4.20%
Associate	0.00%
Other[b]	4.20%

In What Field Was Your Highest Academic Degree?	
Other[c]	66.39%
Evaluation	16.81%
Research	15.13%
Measurement	7.56%
Public administration	5.88%
Organizational development	5.04%
Public policy	3.36%
Public affairs	0.84%

What Percent of Your Income-Earning Time Is Devoted to Evaluation Practice?	
91–100%	39.50%
81–90%	12.61%
71–80%	5.88%
61–70%	3.36%
51–60%	5.88%
41–50%	5.88%
31–40%	5.04%
21–30%	5.88%
11–20%	6.72%
0–10%	7.56%
Not applicable/not currently a practicing evaluator	1.68%

For How Many Years Have You Been or Were You a Practicing Evaluator?	
Over 20 years	35.90%
16–20 years	11.97%
11–15 years	9.40%
6–10 years	18.80%
1–5 years	23.93%

[a]Responses to *Other* included local and county governments, international NGOs, and national education policy boards.
[b]Responses to *Other* included PhD candidates and being self-taught.
[c]Responses to *Other* included anthropology, applied child development, business, change management, chemistry, education, educational leadership, history, industrial & systems engineering, instructional systems technology, international development, marriage & family therapy, political science, psychology, public health, social work, sociology, and urban planning.

Table 6.2. Certification and Credentialing Questions

Indicate Your Level of Agreement Regarding the Following Topics for Evaluators on a Scale of 1–5, With 5 Being Strongly Agree

	1 Strongly Disagree	2	3	4	5 Strongly Agree
A CERTIFICATION system should be implemented	13.38%	17.61%	30.28%	22.54%	16.20%
A CREDENTIALING system should be implemented	14.18%	17.73%	21.28%	26.24%	20.57%
Those currently working as evaluators should be grandparented into being certified/credentialed based on certain criteria	13.04%	12.32%	25.36%	21.74%	27.54%
A system for certified/credentialed evaluators to ensure adherence to ethical and legal guidelines should be implemented	10.14%	5.80%	22.46%	29.71%	31.88%
Certification/credentialing status should be permanent	12.95%	22.30%	33.81%	18.71%	12.23%
Periodic recertification/ recredentialing should be required	10.71%	21.43%	19.29%	35.71%	12.86%

Indicate Your Level of Agreement Regarding Possible Reasons for Having a Certification/Credentialing Process on a Scale of 1–5, With 5 Being Strongly Agree

	1 Strongly Disagree	2	3	4	5 Strongly Agree
Improvement of the quality of the profession	10.22%	6.57%	16.79%	30.66%	35.77%
Standardization of the field	20.59%	16.91%	19.85%	28.68%	13.97%
Protection of consumers	9.56%	5.88%	23.53%	33.82%	27.21%
Image of the profession	9.49%	8.03%	22.63%	33.58%	26.28%
Marketability of evaluators	11.11%	8.89%	22.22%	31.11%	26.67%
None	30.95%	14.29%	26.19%	9.52%	19.05%

somewhat higher than for similar ones in the 1998 survey. (Note: the questions in the two studies were not identical, so the comparison represents an educated estimate on the part of the author.) But more appropriately, taking the highest percentage agreement, the current findings indicate at best that 47% (in regard to credentialing) favor doing something about some type of certification or credentialing. Such findings are informative, but leave considerations of how to proceed quite open.

Respondents had a firm grasp on their evaluation roots in answering other survey questions. They felt that previous evaluation experience should be taken into account when developing a certification/credentialing process, as 49.28% agreed/strongly agreed that those currently working as evaluators should be grandparented into being certified/credentialed based on relevant criteria. The importance of ethics cannot be understated, as 61.59% agreed/strongly agreed that a system for certified/credentialed evaluators to ensure adherence to ethical and legal guidelines should be implemented. Furthermore, the results indicated an emphasis on the need for recertification/recredentialing, as 30.94% agreed/strongly agreed that certification/credentialing status should be permanent versus the 48.57% who agreed/strongly agreed that periodic recertification/recredentialing should be required.

From the open-ended responses to the question soliciting additional comments on evaluator certification or credentialing, those favorable to such an endeavor noted benefits such as the professionalization of the field, the quality of evaluators and the evaluations they would conduct, and the rigor that a certification/credentialing system would establish. As participants stated,

> Evaluation needs to be recognized by the outside world as a separate skill set from other sector or subject expertise. There are too many "experts" conducting evaluations without having the proper training, theory, or real-world grounding, leading to wasted funds and poor advice. Credentialing or certification can help professionalize the field.

> Putting something in place will help with marketing ourselves, improve AEA image and activity level, and reassure clients. This is an essential function of a good professional association.

But on the other hand, unfavorable open-ended responses were notable and cited administrative burdens and potential misuse of the process. One participant summarized the main concerns,

> If you're not certain that the "badge" will improve the quality, effectiveness, and efficiency of program evaluations by an overwhelmingly impressive amount, then don't do it. It will create a web of time-consuming and costly policies, procedures, and hoops to jump through.

Surprisingly, lack of evaluability was also a large concern. One participant noted,

> I can't think of how you could possibly "quantify" evaluator experience and assess the "quality" of this experience without coming up with arbitrary standards and methodologies that intrude upon the evaluator–client relationship in potentially negative ways. The quality of your work as an evaluator determines whether you stay in business as an evaluator.

Adding further to the complex picture, it is important to stress that many respondents remained neutral on the subject. While this may be due somewhat to the inclination or to the natural gravitation toward the median found in many survey scales, it may also indicate the need of evaluators for additional information on certification and credentialing or just that AEA members from the United States are ambivalent about the overall concept. (This may highlight the importance of this issue of New Directions for offering more insight into the topics of accreditation, certification, and credentialing.) Moreover, it points to the groundwork that must be done in terms of communication with members about issues so that if and when they voice opinions and/or make decisions that will be done on the basis of awareness and good information. (This clearly was the case in Canada [Chapter 5 of this issue], where extensive deliberations and interactions occurred prior to any actions being taken on its designation system. Time must be allotted for this type of exchange to ensure that choices are commensurate with the perceptions and views of those ultimately affected by them. This is critical whether it leads to implementing certification or credentialing or it does not. The course the Canadians followed in this regard fits well within the context of AEA.) In the view of one participant,

> I would need a much better background on definitions and purposes of certification and credentialing in order to feel confident about my responses to this survey. I don't know much about the issue.

Participants, both favorable and unfavorable toward certification/credentialing, saw limitations to systems to implement either certification or credentialing. (It is wise to note that although the differences were emphasized upfront in the survey, the two separate yet overlapping ideas [even though there are some major distinctions] of the two forms of status seemed to blend together, they virtually were or appeared to be synonymous to respondents.) A prominent limitation was the increase in bureaucracy and time spent to bring either of the two approaches to life. As an illustration, participants responded that there might be disagreement over what constitutes good evaluation, that certification/credentialing may result in arbitrary rules and regulations, and that the overall goal of ensuring the quality of evaluation work might be lost in the bureaucratic shuffle.

Another limitation was the difficulty in establishing criteria for certification/credentialing and the possible lack of evaluating all programs well. Participants said that

> . . . the professional backgrounds of evaluators vary greatly as do the areas they evaluate. This makes it very complicated in terms of developing a certification/credentialing process.

New Directions for Evaluation • DOI: 10.1002/ev

Program evaluation is not an easily standardized skill because program needs vary across a very wide continuum. It takes years of experience to develop a flexible set of skills and depth of knowledge needed to truly be expert. Passing courses and exams does not make one a good evaluator.

The loss of diversity of practice, along with the possibility of the subsequent narrowing of the evaluation field, was another potential problem as noted by one participant, "One thing that is exciting about evaluation is that it draws people from all disciplines. This may not happen if certification is instituted." From the perspective of another, "The evaluation profession includes an eclectic group of disciplines and individuals. Both certification and credentialing will limit who does the work and reduce the creativity of approaches that are used."

Still another set of concerns was the expense in terms of administrators running a certification/credentialing program, and the costs candidates would incur paying for training and certification/credentialing. Finally, another issue was that a certification/credentialing system may limit evaluators by imposing barriers for new entrants to the field, and by more experienced evaluators possibly being denied certification/credentialing for not meeting certain criteria. One person put it succinctly, "A certification system implies that individuals should not conduct or be restricted from conducting evaluations if they are not certified as an evaluator. It explicitly indicates that someone without a certification is not competent to conduct evaluations when that is not accurate."

Table 6.3 consists of responses to questions about what criteria should be used for awarding certification/credentialing. The criteria for judging evaluators were consistent for both certification and credentialing, with the top three competencies being Working on Evaluation Projects (71.55% agreed or strongly agreed for certification; 70.8% for credentialing), Practicum Experience and/or Design (70.34% agreed or strongly agreed for certification; 70.17% for credentialing), and Courses on Evaluation Content (68.65% agreed/strongly agreed for certification; 69.3% for credentialing). Respondents were of the mind that if experienced evaluators were grandfathered into a certification or credentialing program, the top criteria would be the Portfolio of Work Done by the Individual (63.48% agreed/strongly agreed), a Graduate Degree in Evaluation (61.74%), and the Quality of Evaluation Reports (54.95%). Respondents also favored the same criteria for new evaluators, with 62.5% for a Graduate Degree in Evaluation, 56.49% for the Quality of Evaluation Reports, and 60.71% for the Portfolio of Work Done by the Individual.

In Table 6.4 are the results from questions about governance of the certification/credentialing process. In terms of administering a certification/credentialing program, 41.44% responded that the responsibility should be a joint endeavor between AEA and an independent entity, and 34.23% responded that AEA should be the main administrator of such a program. In

Table 6.3. Criteria for Judging Evaluators for Certification/Credentialing

Indicating Your Level of Agreement Regarding Possible Method for Measuring Competencies Required for Certification/Credentialing on a Scale of 1–5, With 5 Being Strongly Agree

	Certificate					Credentialing				
	5 Strongly Agree	4	3	2	1 Strongly Disagree	5 Strongly Agree	4	3	2	1 Strongly Disagree
Courses on Evaluation Content	34.75%	33.90%	16.95%	10.17%	4.24%	37.72%	31.58%	15.79%	9.65%	5.26%
Practicum Experience and/or Design	38.14%	32.20%	20.34%	4.24%	5.08%	42.98%	27.19%	21.05%	1.75%	7.02%
Qualitative Coursework	26.27%	36.44%	23.73%	8.47%	5.08%	32.46%	31.58%	21.05%	7.89%	7.02%
Quantitative Coursework	25.64%	34.86%	21.37%	9.40%	5.13%	32.46%	32.46%	19.30%	8.77%	7.02%
Conference Workshop	9.32%	31.36%	33.05%	13.56%	12.71%	14.29%	28.57%	28.57%	15.18%	13.39%
Other Professional Development	12.28%	34.21%	35.96%	9.65%	7.89%	16.22%	32.43%	31.53%	9.91%	9.91%
Work on Evaluation Projects	44.83%	26.72%	15.52%	6.90%	6.03%	44.25%	26.55%	16.81%	5.31%	7.08%
Conducting Evaluation Research	30.77%	23.92%	20.51%	11.97%	12.82%	30.97%	25.66%	15.93%	11.50%	15.93%
Publishing Evaluation Related Articles	13.79%	17.24%	27.59%	18.10%	23.28%	14.91%	19.30%	21.93%	16.67%	27.19%
Involvement in Evaluation Organization	15.52%	19.83%	31.03%	15.52%	18.10%	21.62%	20.72%	27.03%	10.81%	19.82%

(Continued)

Table 6.3. Continued

Indicate Your Level of Agreement Regarding Criteria for Awarding Certification/Credentialing Grandparenting Status to Established Evaluators and to New Evaluators on a Scale of 1–5, With 5 Being Strongly Agree

	Grandparenting to Established Evaluators					New Evaluators				
	5 Strongly Agree	4	3	2	1 Strongly Disagree	5 Strongly Agree	4	3	2	1 Strongly Disagree
AEA Membership	20.35%	18.58%	19.47%	11.50%	30.09%	15.18%	17.86%	20.54%	16.96%	29.46%
Graduate Degree in Evaluation Related Discipline	31.58%	28.95%	21.05%	5.26%	13.16%	30.91%	30.91%	20.00%	5.54%	12.73%
Graduate Degree in Evaluation	34.78%	26.96%	14.78%	6.96%	16.52%	37.50%	25.00%	13.39%	8.04%	16.07%
Leadership in Evaluation Organizations	15.79%	22.81%	21.05%	17.54%	22.81%	8.93%	13.39%	27.68%	23.21%	26.79%
Letters in Recommendation	11.30%	30.43%	27.83%	13.04%	17.39%	15.32%	27.93%	24.32%	17.12%	15.32%
Minimal Year of Evaluation Work	28.70%	33.91%	20.00%	8.70%	8.70%	25.33%	25.33%	26.13%	12.61%	10.81%
Other Certification Related to the Evaluated Field	16.36%	19.09%	38.18%	9.09%	17.27%	12.84%	28.44%	31.19%	7.34%	20.18%
Portfolio of Work Done by the Individual	40.87%	22.61%	19.13%	6.09%	11.30%	34.82%	25.89%	21.43%	7.14%	10.71%
Postgraduate Evaluation Education	23.10%	31.86%	23.89%	7.96%	13.27%	24.32%	27.03%	27.03	8.11%	13.51%
Presentations at Evaluation Conferences	14.78%	19.13%	20.87%	23.48%	21.74%	13.39%	20.54%	25.00%	17.86%	23.21%
Presentations at Nonevaluation Conferences	10.43%	13.91%	22.61%	23.96%	26.09%	10.91%	16.36%	25.45%	19.09%	28.18%
Publications in Evaluation Journals	18.42%	19.30%	21.05%	18.42%	22.81%	12.73%	19.09%	26.36%	16.36%	25.54%
Publications in Nonevaluation Journals	15.79%	10.53%	28.07%	21.05%	24.56%	10.00%	13.64%	26.36%	20.00%	30.00%
Quality of Evaluation Reports	32.43%	22.52%	19.82%	9.91%	15.32%	21.30%	21.30%	23.15%	7.41%	12.96%

Table 6.4. Governance of the Certification/Credentialing Process

In Your Opinion, Who Should Be Responsible for Administering a Certification/ Credentialing Program?

Joint endeavor by AEA and an independent entity	41.44%
AEA	34.23%
Other[a]	15.32%
Independent entity	9.01%

In Your Opinion, Who Should Cover the Costs Associated With a Certification/ Credentialing Program?

Combination of AEA and candidates	48.67%
Certification/credentialing candidates	27.43%
Other[b]	12.39%
AEA	11.50%

If a Certification or Credentialing System Were in Place That Required Candidates to Pay a Fee, How Much Would You Be Willing to Pay for Such a Service?

UP to $100	34.23%
$101–$200	40.54%
$201–$300	18.02%
Over $300	18.92%

[a]Responses to *Other* included AEA and a consortium of evaluation societies, AEA and educational institutions, an AEA-sponsored certification committee composed of recognized leaders in many different fields, and university-accredited programs.
[b]Responses to *Other* included a combination of an independent entity and candidates, and a combination of AEA, universities, and candidates.

the 1998 survey, 73% of respondents said that AEA should be the main administrator, with 22% favoring an independent agency in charge of program administration. These numbers show a move toward collaboration among entities, or from another point of view they denote the difficulties inherent in going forward with certification and what it might take to do so. Additionally, 48.67% responded that the costs of administering such a program should be taken on by a combination of AEA and the candidates for certification/credentialing, and 27.43% stated that the candidates themselves should bear the cost. This is similar to the 1998 findings in which 56% responded that the costs should be handled by a combination of AEA and candidates, and 39% saw this responsibility resting upon the shoulders of the candidates themselves, they should bear the cost.

Conclusions

A major conclusion is that the pattern from the previous U.S. survey was generally repeated more than 16 years later. AEA members in the United States are mixed on the propositions of certification and credentialing and probably have the same view of accreditation. There are a plethora of perceptions as to whether there is value in making any decisions about them at the present time or only in proceeding after a considerable period is devoted to working with the organizational membership. More awareness and discussion are in order, and some years will have to be devoted to obtain a deeper picture of what U.S. evaluators are thinking about and why they see things in so many different ways.

A second conclusion that may be drawn from these results is the disparity of views regarding the assessment of evaluators themselves in order to qualify for certification or credentialing. It is interesting to note that those participants who felt a certification and/or credentialing program should be implemented provided examples of evaluands, criteria, and implementation ideas. To support their points, participants referenced the Joint Committee on Standards for Educational Evaluation (JCSEE), the American Psychological Association (APA), and the National Board for Certified Counselors (NBCC) standards as potential building blocks for an evaluation certification or credentialing program. They were thinking like an evaluator taking on a new project, in that they formulated criteria upon which a certification or credentialing program should be established along with many possible ways of evaluating such an endeavor.

Similarly, those participants who were on the other side of the issue seemed to have difficulty conceiving of a potential evaluation of themselves as reflected in the comment, "I just don't see how an 'outside' credentialing or certification authority could adequately and accurately assess the quality of an evaluation practitioner's work without being there during the evaluation." Evaluators gladly take on work on many complex issues, but when it becomes that of evaluating evaluators, they are unable to fathom such an endeavor. (This might not be the most surprising of findings.)

Third, the interdisciplinary nature of the evaluation field may also present a quandary to thinking about certification and/or credentialing. While this has been beneficial to evaluation in infusing it with a vast array of disciplines (energy, government, education, for-profit and nonprofit entities, human resource development, and economics), the large variability in itself poses a very large challenge for how we might go about certifying or credentialing.

- Is one overall certification/credentialing system sufficient?
- Should there be several levels of certification/credentialing?
- Does the specific content area (energy, education, government, etc.) in which evaluators work warrant its own certificate/credential?

(For example, some of the content such as the accountability emphasis in the field of education may limit the scope and nature of what evaluators do in their jobs.)

A fourth interesting conclusion is the need for evaluation entities (such as AEA or other independent bodies or groups) to work with universities to offer more degrees specifically in evaluation. (See Chapter 3 of this issue, for how the preparation of evaluators has evolved and is continuing to do so over the past 20 years or so.) Survey respondents agreed or strongly agreed that coursework on evaluation content and graduate degrees in evaluation are important criteria for certifying/credentialing—both for experienced evaluators and new evaluators. While there are some university programs that offer degrees in evaluation, they are comparatively few (American Evaluation Association, n.d.a), although the sheer number of programs offering evaluation content seems to be increasing as observed in a recent study (LaVelle, 2014).

Most current graduate work in evaluation includes concentrations in evaluation or research, with the overall degree being in another field such as sociology or anthropology. As evidence of this point, 66.39% of respondents indicated that their degree was in a field *other* than evaluation. If having a degree in evaluation is important to the certification/credentialing process, then universities should offer more degrees in evaluation to accommodate that demand. This implies that what constitutes a program and what is meant by the preparation of evaluators is in need of more attention. Obviously this would have ties to the concern about the accreditation of programs.

A fifth conclusion is the requirement for any certification/credentialing governance to include training on legal and ethical issues as pertaining to evaluation. Survey results indicated that 61.59% of respondents agreed/strongly agreed that a system for certified/credentialed evaluators to ensure adherence to legal and ethical guidelines should be implemented. Over the past several years, AEA has created much training and information targeting ethical issues (AEA, n.d.b), and many journal articles have focused on ethical scenarios for evaluators. While embedding information on legal and ethical guidance for evaluators in certification/credentialing programs would be relatively easy, the challenge is to weave that information into a fair and equitable governance system that would help evaluators and the clients they serve. That is a more subtle proposition especially the part about enhancing the awareness of consumers and clients.

Sixth, it would be important to reiterate that AEA members should have more information about the entire certification/credentialing issue before being able to make considered choices, and this would of necessity extend to the processes for granting such status and what kind of system would have to be established. While a lot of respondents had definite feelings favoring or opposing certification/credentialing, there were many neutral responses. It is clear that more information on what certification and credentialing mean for professional evaluators professionally and to the broader evaluation community is needed.

- How will certification/credentialing affect an evaluator's relationship with various organizations and society at large?

- All else being equal, is there a distinct advantage or difference between an evaluator who is certified/credentialed and one who is not?
- How can those advantages/differences be effectively promoted internal and external to the evaluation community?
- What is the appropriate leadership and governance needed for the certification/credentialing process?
- Moreover, who evaluates the evaluator and who decides about the granting of the certificate or credential with its conveyed status?

Respondents additionally noted the possible political bias or other preferential treatment in how the process is conducted. Procedures would need to take these and other issues (grandfathering experienced evaluators, ensuring ethical and legal guidelines for evaluation are adhered to, recertifying/recredentialing periodically) into account to create a fair, efficient process that benefits the evaluation community.

Further study and work are necessary to investigate the potential for a future certification or credentialing system for evaluators. Researchers could extend this exploratory survey to the entire AEA membership within the United States to obtain a clearer picture of the viability of a certification or credentialing system. More and more probing questions would be useful. In-depth interviews of a cross-section of evaluators (those new to the field and old hands) to learn more about their thoughts and insights into these critical issues in accreditation, certification, and credentialing would also be important.

Much could be gained by researchers surveying those who employ or otherwise hire evaluators to discover the skills that are most important to those entities and whether a certification/credentialing program could assist with providing employers what they need. Future work could focus on whether to have one or more certification/credentialing systems based on discipline (education, social work, public policy, and others) and what would be appropriate standards for awarding certificates.

It is abundantly clear that much must be done before decisions are made to proceed one way or the other as to which path is chosen (certifying/credentialing or maintaining the status quo). Hopefully, this chapter and volume will generate a much-needed discussion of ways to further evaluation and ensure that quality evaluations are the earmark of the field. Such time and attention may be of value not only to the evaluation community but also to the overall society as people in many different fields and disciplines make data-driven decisions to improve their projects and programs.

References

Altschuld, J. W. (1999). The certification of evaluators: Highlights from a report submitted to the board of directors of the American Evaluation Association. *American Journal of Evaluation, 20*(3), 481–493. doi:10.1177/109821409902000307

Altschuld, J. W., Baron, M., Engle, M., Hung, H., King, J. A., Kuji-Shikatani, K.,...
Stevahn, L. (2012). *Evaluator credentialing and certification revisited: Where have we come in the last decade?* Think tank presented at the 2012 Annual Conference of the American Evaluation Association, Minneapolis, MN.

American Evaluation Association (AEA). (n.d.a). *University programs.* Retrieved from http://www.eval.org/p/cm/ld/fid=43

American Evaluation Association (AEA). (n.d.b). *AEA guiding principles training package.* Retrieved from http://www.eval.org/p/cm/ld/fid=105

American Evaluation Association (AEA). (2012). *26th Annual Conference of the American Evaluation Association.* Retrieved from http://archive.eval.org/eval2012/default.asp

American Evaluation Association (AEA). (2013). *27th Annual Conference of the American Evaluation Association.* Retrieved from http://www.eval.org/Evaluation2013

American Evaluation Association (AEA). (2014). *28th Annual Conference of the American Evaluation Association.* Retrieved from http://www.eval.org/p/cm/ld/fid=226

Bickman, L. (1999). AEA, bold or timid? *American Journal of Evaluation, 20*(3), 519–520. doi:10.1177/109821409902000310

Jones, S. C., & Worthen, B. R. (1999). AEA members' opinions concerning evaluator certification. *American Journal of Evaluation, 20*(3), 495–506. doi:10.1177/109821409902000308

King, J. A. (2012, April). *Credentialing: Identifying the core vs. specialized competencies* [AEA Thought Leaders Discussion Forum]. Retrieved from http://comm.eval.org/EVAL/Discussions/DigestViewer/?GroupId=91

LaVelle, J. M. (2014). *An analysis of evaluation education programs and evaluator skills across the world* (Doctoral dissertation). Claremont Graduate University, Claremont, CA.

Stevahn, L., King, J. A., Ghere, G., & Minnema, J. (2005). Establishing essential competencies for program evaluators. *American Journal of Evaluation, 26*(1), 43–59. doi:10.1177/1098214004273180

Worthen, B. R. (1999). Critical challenges confronting certification of evaluators. *American Journal of Evaluation, 20*(3), 533–555. doi:10.1177/109821409902000312

MICHELLE BARON SEIDLING is an evaluation and training strategist based in Minneapolis, Minnesota.

7

Accreditation, Certification, Credentialing: Does It Help?

Gene Shackman

Abstract

The content and discussion of the first six chapters along with some key literature provide the basis upon which the author formulates his views about accreditation, certification, and credentialing. His position is that anything done would have to lead to better evaluations, and at present there is insufficient evidence about whether accreditation, certification, and credentialing would do so. Thus, the main goal now is to gather further evidence. © Wiley Periodicals, Inc., and the American Evaluation Association.

I n this chapter, I will review literature about the pros and cons of accreditation, certification, and credentialing (ACC) for evaluators. This topic has come up many times over the years (Altschuld & Engle, Chapter 1 of this issue), and more than a few organizations have some kind of credentialing system (Canadian Evaluation Society [CES]) or are considering one (Bustello, 2013; IDEAS Working Group on Evaluation Competencies, 2012; UK Evaluation Society, 2013). In addition, I will provide a summary about ACC in evaluation as well as in other fields to see how the conclusions drawn about ACC for them relate to those for us.

I'll start by saying that the major reason for having evaluators be certified or credentialed or going to accredited programs is to ensure that such actions lead to better outcomes for target populations. Social, economic, education, or health programs that are evaluated by certified or credentialed professionals should have better outcomes than do programs evaluated by people who do not have such qualifications. For example, clients in a jobs program should be more likely to get jobs, or clients in a drug prevention program should be less likely to use drugs, if their programs were evaluated by certified or credentialed evaluators. Presumably, those with the appropriate status/designation should be better able to evaluate a program or project (how well it is working, what elements in it contribute to its goals, what isn't contributing) and to make suggestions on how to improve it than do others who did not have the status. Certified or credentialed evaluators should have more in-depth professional preparation in research methods, evaluation strategies, and in conveying results to decision makers. They should have greater understanding of how to deal with politics and so should be better able to get recommendations implemented. Another reason for ACC might be whether they demonstrated (proved) to be beneficial in helping employers and the public select a qualified professional.

I also state, at the beginning of this chapter, that the conclusion being offered here is that for the most part there is insufficient evidence about whether ACC results in positive outcomes. A search of sources, including Google Scholar and several evaluation journals,[1] found a number of reviews and studies, most of which concluded that there is simply insufficient evidence to support a stance one way or the other about any of the three topics (ACC) at the current time.

All of the conclusions about ACC in evaluation are generally the same for ACC in other professions. Like evaluation, the conclusion from many areas and disciplines is that there is insufficient research about whether ACC is worthwhile.

Thus, it is appropriate to suggest that the main and prominent job of evaluation and of other professions is to investigate whether ACC does result in better outcomes for program participants. I want to emphasize that while I see the main usefulness of the three entities in that light, others view the situation differently and offer other reasons for the importance of ACC.

The six chapters in this issue, besides this one, describe certification, credentialing, and accreditation quite well and in some depth, so it is not necessary to do so here. Rather, I will capitalize on what those chapter authors have described. Since elements in ACC overlap, the three processes will be treated somewhat interchangeably.

Certification, Credentialing, and Accreditation in Evaluation

Morra Imas (2010) looked at the development and use of competencies for evaluators. Her review included a table showing reasons in support of and arguments against competencies and certification or credentialing (Table 7.1). It offers a good backdrop for considering the arguments for

Table 7.1. Competency Frameworks: Arguments For and Against

COMMON ARGUMENTS IN SUPPORT OF COMPETENCY FRAMEWORKS

Increase credibility of the evaluation function as a profession and increase recognition of evaluation staff as professionals
Increase consistency and methodological rigor within the evaluation community
Increase available training
Increase the skills of those in the evaluation community as more training becomes available to complement the competencies
Decrease barriers to entry and broaden the talent pool
Promote self-responsibility for continuing improvement of evaluation skills
Provide a basis for selecting or procuring the services of evaluators
Provide a basis for developing education and training programs
Promote ethical code of practice

*ADDITIONAL ARGUMENTS IN SUPPORT OF CERTIFICATION
OR CREDENTIALING SYSTEMS*

Show that one has successfully demonstrated knowledge, skills, training, and experience to an independent board and that one abides by a code of ethics
Provide prestige
Provide incentives by enhancing marketability and salaries
Provide a basis for disciplining those who do not follow ethical codes or who misrepresent their capabilities and/or experience
Avoid narrow competency definitions that may be self-serving to specific organizations
Help prevent poorly qualified persons practicing the profession from undermining the public trust and confidence

COMMON ARGUMENTS IN OPPOSITION TO COMPETENCY FRAMEWORKS

No empirical evidence that specific competencies are necessary or critical to the practice of the profession in all contexts
No evidence that consistency in backgrounds and experience is desirable for the profession
Not enough available education or training programs to provide the required skills to all
Competency statements cannot keep up with a rapidly changing profession
Given the diversity of contexts in which the evaluation profession is practiced, no one set of competencies can be specified or agreed to
Cost of education and training and access to education and training serve as barriers to entry
Given the diversity of contexts in which the evaluation profession is practiced, no one individual can meet all the required competencies
What is most important to evaluation—the attitudes and disposition of the evaluator—cannot be measured

*ADDITIONAL ARGUMENTS IN OPPOSITION TO CERTIFICATION
OR CREDENTIALING SYSTEMS*

Promotes exclusivity
Works unfairly against those who have learned primarily through doing and have years of experience but little formal training
Little assurance that there would be consistency in application across certifying/credentialing groups
Sufficient competition exists in the workplace and efforts to guide, constrain, or regulate the profession are not necessary
Education and training programs should be accredited; certification or credentialing of individuals is not needed
Certification and credentialing systems cannot prevent poor practice from those holding certificates or credentials, nor do those graduating from accredited programs necessarily have the skills and knowledge needed
Does not adequately recognize alternate forms of education, such as mentoring, coaching, and twinning

Source: Morra Imas (2010). Used with Permission (personal communication 2014).

NEW DIRECTIONS FOR EVALUATION • DOI: 10.1002/ev

and against ACC. Some of the advantages for certification and competencies include:

- increasing the credibility of the evaluation profession and enhancing the recognition of evaluators as professionals,
- improving consistency and methodological rigor,
- increasing availability of training,
- demonstrating acquisition of knowledge/experience, and
- providing a means of identifying those who *don't* have the requisite background.

On the other side of the ledger, reasons against ACC include:

- lack of evidence that use of competencies is critical to conduct evaluations,
- that certification cannot prevent poor practice from those holding certificates,
- costs of training and education,
- difficulty in agreeing on one set of competencies, and
- that the latter change over time as the profession changes.

It is of value to note that there is almost equivalent weighting for the advantages and disadvantages for all of the above propositions, and the arguments for the most part are given on logical grounds and not on empirical ones.

Hwalek (2011) recently considered how certification might fit evaluators in the federal government. Several of the features she described are similar to those of Morra Imas. For example, she indicated that certification would mean that evaluators would all have to have the agreed-upon program evaluation education, competencies, and experiences, and might also have to keep their knowledge current through continuing education. The authors of the other chapters brought up closely related points (King & Stevahn, Chapter 2 of this issue). Even further, Altschuld and Engle (Chapter 1 of this issue) wrote that evaluation has worked for many years without any formalized, universally agreed on set of competencies, or without certification, so some may question why certification or a consensus list of competencies is needed. Hwalek raised a concern akin to one noted by Morra Imas that certification could also be used to differentiate evaluators from other professionals who might do related work.

Picciotto (2011) added what may be implied in Morra Imas's table but is not specifically stated that professional certification can be expensive, and that there may be many questions about the reliability of assessment of professional competencies. The cost of becoming credentialed by the CES, for example, is around $500, and may take up to 36 months to complete (website of Canadian Evaluation Society Professional Designations Program, n.d.). There are no data yet on the reliability of the credentialing process and who would or should bear the financial burden for becoming and maintaining a designation. In a profession with many part-time evaluators, such questions have to be raised and deliberated.

Picciotto (2011) noted the issue of whether evaluators were in favor of certification and commented that two thirds of European Evaluation Society members indicated that certification was not a priority. One survey in the late 1990s found that about half of the members of the American Evaluation Association (AEA) were in favor of certification, but half were not (Altschuld & Engle, Chapter 1 of this issue). Kuji-Shikatani (Chapter 5 of this issue) wrote that when the CES initially offered credentialing, only 10% of the members participated at first and as of a slightly later date (Kuji-Shikatani) the percentage had risen to about 14%. Seidling (Chapter 6 of this issue) reported on a 2014 survey of AEA members that obtained mixed results. First, only about 15% of those contacted responded to the survey. Of those who did, about 39% agreed that a certification system should be implemented, and about 47% agreed that a credentialing system should be implemented. In both cases, more than half of respondents were indifferent or disagreed.

A critical concern about the practicality of ACC is the education required for the certificate or credential. It would be reasonable that there should be some degree of agreement about the preparation people should receive and master in order to obtain the status implied by being certified or credentialed. If there were established and adhered to criteria on methods for conducting evaluations and programs to prepare evaluators in their use, then ACC should enhance consistency and methodological rigor of evaluations. In this regard, LaVelle and Donaldson (Chapter 3 of this issue) provide an overview of training options for evaluators in the United States and the world and show that the preparation seems to be fairly uniform across the many different schools that have an evaluation-specific masters' track.

On the other hand, the above writers found that the picture was much more varied in doctoral level programs, and that educational opportunities are more diverse than they had been in the past. They thought there is still much work to be done on understanding how evaluators obtain formal and informal preparation for entering the profession. Kuji-Shikatani (Chapter 5 of this issue) described the CES experience, noting that the CES has an officially sponsored Essential Skills Series. However, the series is not extensive and only guarantees a very basic level of knowledge (J. W. Altschuld, personal communication, 2014). Nonetheless, because CES has the essential skills courses it appears a little easier for the organization to establish a credentialing system.

All of the positions for and against ACC should, theoretically, be based on whether they lead to the evaluation outcomes described earlier. If so, then certification and credentialing could help potential clients to select evaluators. Clients and potential clients may not fully comprehend ACC, but presumably they would prefer to choose evaluators who are certified or credentialed, or who went to accredited institutions.

The issues now being discussed are pretty much the same ones that have been looked since the 1970s. More recently, Halpern (2005) posited that certification and/or credentialing can help establish evaluation as a profession with evaluators as professionals who follow certain standards and codes of behavior. ACC may be useful in differentiating those who have the basic set of evaluation competencies from those who don't but may still claim they can do evaluation.

About 15 years ago, Altschuld (1999) created a similar table to the one of Morra Imas about the pros and cons of certification. For him the positives were along the same lines—professionalization, increased educational opportunities, ensuring a minimum level of competency, and safeguards for the public. One major area of negatives he dealt with in detail was the complexity of the certification and/or credentialing process. In this vein, Morra Imas implied that certification could raise costs to join evaluation associations and costs of evaluation for consumers. Finally, Altschuld (1999) mentioned resistance by evaluation association members, in tune with the concern brought up by Picciotto (2011).

Certification, Credentialing, and Accreditation Outside of Evaluation

The issues discussed in the field of evaluation are akin to those for ACC in other fields. Foster (2012) cited professionalization through recognition of specialized education, knowledge and skills, and public protection in a review about counseling. Shook and Johnston (2011) indicated that having credentials is a common way for applied behavior analysis professionals to demonstrate to the public that they have met recognized standards of competence in their field, and that the public uses such credentials as a way to identify those who are at least minimally competent. Allegrante, Barry, Auld and Lamarre (2012) see credentialing as part of a process to improve the capabilities of health education professionals. Rollinson (2011) writes that, more broadly, credentialing demonstrates expertise or understanding of a standard body of knowledge.

Outside of evaluation, there are reviews about certification and whether it helps to improve outcomes in other professions. The results are somewhat mixed, but mainly there is insufficient evidence to draw a conclusion or take a position as to whether it makes a difference. Analogously, a few studies and reviews indicate that there is not enough support to warrant a conclusion about whether accreditation helps; that view is echoed in the chapter by McDavid and Huse (Chapter 4 of this issue).

In contrast, two articles did find better outcomes associated with ACC. Curry, Eckles, Stuart, Schneider-Muñoz, and Qaqish (2013) observed that certified child and youth practitioners receive higher performance ratings from their supervisors than noncertified practitioners, after accounting for the effects of race, gender, education, experience, and certification exam results (pass/fail). Curtis et al. (2009) wrote that performing an implantable cardioverter-defibrillator (ICD) procedure by cardiologists not certified in that specific procedure was associated with a higher risk of procedural complications when compared with the procedure performed by a certified cardiologist.

By contrast, most reviews come to the conclusion that there is just no way to judge the effects of certifying or credentialing practitioners. In fact, there are some reviews that suggest that these procedures make no difference or do not protect against incompetence. We simply do not know.

In a brief literature review, Krapohl, Manojlovich, Redman, and Zhang (2010) stated that there was yet little research about whether certified and noncertified nurses differed in their clinical practice. In their study, there was not a significant relationship between the proportion of certified nurses on a unit and patient outcomes. Lengnick-Hall and Aguinis (2012) were of the same opinion when they stated that there was no evidence yet on the impact HR certification may have on any important individual- and organizational-level outcomes. And Hickey et al. (2013) chimed in about the limited research on whether credentialing leads to higher quality of care, more uniform practice, and better patient outcomes. Starkweather and Stevenson (2011) found no difference in project success rates between project managers who were Project Management Professional (PMP®)-certified and those who were not. Ulmer (2010) reported that manufacturing companies having certified employees did not do significantly better at quality cost improvement or waste cost reduction than companies that did not have such personnel.

Buscemi, Wang, Phy, and Nugent (2012) suggested that research does not provide strong backing for the benefits of board certification for internal medicine, but that lack of support may relate to the quality of the research that was conducted and in turn to the conclusions that were drawn from the study. Gurgacz, Smith, Truskett, Babidge, and Maddern (2012) reported that a literature search did not uncover studies linking credentialing of surgeons to clinical safety and patient outcomes.

Moving to accreditation, one investigation observed that it makes no difference in clinical practice (Shaw et al., 2014) and another study reported that it resulted in worse outcomes at cancer centers (Merkow, Chung, Paruch, Bentrem, & Bilimoria, 2014). One review underscored that it is not yet known whether accreditation has an impact on medical center outcomes (Boulet & van Zanten, 2014). McDavid and Huse (Chapter 4 of this issue) mention a potential problem with accreditation sometimes discussed in the literature, in that institutions in the process of seeking or maintaining accreditation may focus on meeting external standards rather than working toward innovation, or coming up with creative solutions to problems. In other words the focus is on the status quo with little room for ideas of creativeness and institutional change. They describe a potential problem for certification, credentialing, and accreditation: the difficulty in coming to agreement about necessary competencies.

Returning to certification, one paper, unfortunately noted that the motive for it was aligned to being more employable, rather than to improve the quality of services (Clark, 2013). According to Clark, the job market in pharmacy is tightening, so certification is used as a way to demonstrate clinical knowledge, and thus being more attractive to employers. While it certainly makes sense to pursue certification to increase the chance of employment, its primary goal still should be improving quality of services.

Conclusions

The first conclusion is that there is insufficient evidence to indicate whether ACC will improve program outcomes. Obviously, the most convincing studies would be to compare outcomes from programs that were evaluated by people with certification, credentials, or who attended an accredited preparation program, to outcomes from programs that were evaluated by people who were not certified or credentialed, or who did not attend an accredited program.

Recently, the CES instituted credentialing, so there may be some possibility of using their experience to evaluate credentialing. Research could, as described above, compare outcomes of programs evaluated by those with and without credentials. However, there are difficulties with such research. For example, people self-select into applying for credentials, so we don't have any unbiased control and experimental groups. There are statistical methods that might help to account for bias in the experimental and control situations such as propensity score analysis (PSA) or categorical and regression tree analysis (CART). PSA essentially looks for ways to adjust so there are comparable experimental and control groups (Environmental Protection Agency, 2012), and CART does not make any assumptions about whether people are randomly or normally distributed (Statsoft, 2013).

Research could also use a retrospective method, asking evaluators or clients to compare how the evaluations are being done now versus how they were done a few years ago. There are many flaws with assigning causality from this approach, but it would tend to give some useful information.

Research could also be used in another way, in process evaluation. Evaluators and clients could be asked about how well an evaluation is being conducted, how it might be improved, whether it provided useful information, and whether the evaluator respected the rights of, and paid attention to the needs of, the client. This is not an evaluation of ACC, but could help provide insights about how qualified professionals conducted the evaluation, whether they adhered to the standards expected by credentialed or certified evaluators.

A second conclusion from this review is that it appears there is not overwhelming support for ACC among evaluators. As mentioned, only a small percent of Canadian evaluators applied for the credentialing process, and only a small percent of AEA members responded to the survey about ACC. Thus, a main job of evaluation associations is to probe more deeply into whether their members want ACC, what they expect from it, and whether it can meet those expectations. Or even better yet, if more professionalization of the field is desired, what are ways that the associations can go about facilitating that outcome. To reiterate, the conclusions described above are very much like those about ACC in a number of other fields: there is insufficient evidence about whether ACC leads to better outcomes, so more research is needed.

Finally, I want to make clear that lack of evidence about whether ACC has any impact on outcomes is not the same as saying that it does not have any impact. The position taken in this chapter is simply that there isn't enough research at this time to determine whether ACC does have an impact. The question remains about whether ACC results in better evaluations and in turn outcomes, especially for the groups and individuals that receive the benefits of programs and projects. If we can demonstrate that our efforts enhance the benefits, then accreditation, certification, and credentialing are worthwhile.

Note

1. *American Journal of Evaluation, Canadian Journal of Evaluation, Journal of MultiDisciplinary Evaluation.*

References

Allegrante, J. P., Barry, M. M., Auld, M. E., & Lamarre, M. C. (2012). Galway revisited: Tracking global progress in core competencies and quality assurance for health education and health promotion. *Health Education & Behavior, 39*(6), 643–647.

Altschuld, J. W. (1999). The certification of evaluators: Highlights from a report submitted to the board of directors of the American Evaluation Association. *American Journal of Evaluation, 20*(3), 481–493.

Boulet, J., & van Zanten, M. (2014). Ensuring high-quality patient care: The role of accreditation, licensure, specialty certification and revalidation in medicine. *Medical Education, 48*(1), 75–86.

Buscemi, D., Wang, H., Phy, M., & Nugent, K. (2012). Maintenance of certification in internal medicine: Participation rates and patient outcomes. *Journal of Community Hospital Internal Medicine Perspectives, 2*(4), 19753. Retrieved from http://dx.doi.org/10.3402/jchimp.v2i4.19753

Bustello, M. (2013, September). A message from the President. *Evaluation Connections: The European Evaluation Society Newsletter*, 1–2. Retrieved from http://www.europeanevaluation.org/resources/connections

Canadian Evaluation Society Professional Designations Program. (n.d.). Retrieved from http://old.evaluationcanada.ca/site.cgi?s=50&ss=3&_lang=en

Clark, T. R. (2013). Credentialing in pharmacy—An overview. *The Consultant Pharmacist, 28*(1), 24–29.

Curry, D., Eckles, F., Stuart, C., Schneider-Muñoz, A. J., & Qaqish, B. (2013). National certification for child and youth workers: Does it make a difference? *Children and Youth Services Review, 35*(11), 1795–1800.

Curtis, J. P., Luebbert, J. J., Wang, Y., Rathore, S. S., Chen, J., Heidenrich, P. A., ... Krumholz, H. M. (2009). Association of physician certification and outcomes among patients receiving an implantable cardioverter-defibrillator. *JAMA, 301*(16), 1661–1670. doi:10.1001/jama.2009.547

Environmental Protection Agency. (2012). *Propensity score analysis. CADDIS: The Causal Analysis/Diagnosis Decision Information System.* Retrieved from http://www.epa.gov/caddis/index.html

Foster, L. H. (2012). Professional counselor credentialing and program accreditation in the United States: A historical review. *Journal for International Counselor Education, 4*, 42–56.

Gurgacz, S. L., Smith, J. A., Truskett, P. G., Babidge, W. J., & Maddern, G. J. (2012). Credentialing of surgeons: A systematic review across a number of jurisdictions. *ANZ Journal of Surgery, 82*, 492–498.

Halpern, G. (2005, October). In favour of the certification of evaluators. In A. Love (Chair), *Evaluator certification debate: Canadian and American views.* Debate conducted at the meeting of the Canadian Evaluation Society and the American Evaluation Association, Toronto, Onterio. Retrieved from http://evaluationcanada.ca/distribution/20051027_halpern_gerald.pdf

Hickey, J. V., Unruh, L. R., Newhouse, R. P., Koithan, M., Johantgen, M. E., Hughes, R. G., ... Lundmark, V. A. (2013). Credentialing: The need for a national research agenda. *Nursing Outlook, 62*(2), 119–127.

Hwalek, M. (2011). The stars are aligned for disruptive change in evaluation practice. *American Journal of Evaluation, 32*(4), 582–584.

IDEAS Working Group on Evaluation Competencies. (2012). *Competencies for development evaluation evaluators, managers, and commissioners.* Retrieved from http://www.ideas-int.org/documents/file_list.cfm?DocsSubCatID=48

Krapohl, G., Manojlovich, M., Redman, R., & Zhang, L. (2010). Nursing specialty certification and nursing-sensitive patient outcomes in the intensive care unit. *American Journal of Critical Care, 19*(6), 490–498.

Lengnick-Hall, M. L., & Aguinis, H. (2012). What is the value of human resource certification? A multi-level framework for research. *Human Resource Management Review, 22*(4), 246–257.

Merkow, R. P., Chung, J. W., Paruch, J. L., Bentrem, D. J., & Bilimoria, K. (2014). Relationship between cancer center accreditation and performance on publicly reported quality measures. *Annals of Surgery, 259*(6), 1091–1097.

Morra Imas, L. G. (2010, May). *The movement for global competencies for development evaluators.* Paper presented at the meeting of the Canadian Evaluation Society, Victoria, BC. Retrieved from http://www.ideas-int.org/documents/docs/The%20Movement%20for%20Global%20Comptencies%20for%20Development%20Evaluators1.pdf

Picciotto, R. (2011). The logic of evaluation professionalism. *Evaluation, 17*(2), 165–180.

Rollinson, R. (2011). Should strategy professionals be certified? *Strategy & Leadership, 39*(1), 39–43.

Shaw, C. D., Groene, O., Botje, D., Sunol, R., Kutryba, B., Klazinga, N., ... Wagner, C. on behalf of the DUQuE Project Consortium. (2014). The effect of certification and accreditation on quality management in 4 clinical services in 73 European hospitals. *International Journal for Quality in Health Care, 26*(1), 100–107. Advanced online publication. doi:10.1093/intqhc/mzu023

Shook, G., & Johnston, J. (2011). Training and professional certification in applied behavioral analysis. In W. W. Fisher, C. C. Piazza, & H. S. Roane. (Eds.), *Handbook of applied behavior analysis* (pp. 498–510). New York, NY: Guilford Press.

Starkweather, J., & Stevenson, D. H. (2011). PMP® certification as a core competency: Necessary but not sufficient. *Project Management Journal, 42*(1), 31–41.

StatSoft, Inc. (2013). *Electronic statistics textbook.* Tulsa, OK: StatSoft. Retrieved from http://www.statsoft.com/textbook/

UK Evaluation Society. (2013). *Voluntary Evaluator Peer Review VEPR system.* Retrieved from http://www.evaluation.org.uk/news/article/Voluntary-Evaluator-Peer-Review-VEPR-system

Ulmer, J. M. (2010). Professional certification: A study of significance. *Journal of Industrial Technology, 26*(2), 2–11. Retrieved from http://c.ymcdn.com/sites/www.atmae.org/resource/resmgr/Articles/ulmer032610.pdf

GENE SHACKMAN, an applied sociologist, is the founder and director of the Global Social Change Research Project and manages the website "Free Resources for Program Evaluation and Social Research Methods."

INDEX

A

AACSB. *See* Association to Advance Collegiate Schools of Business (AACSB)

AACSB Standards for Business Accreditation, 56

Accreditation, 53–66; for accounting education, 60–61; background, 55–59; benefits of, 59; for business management education, 60; critical perspectives on, 63–65; critical theory on, 64–65; definition of, 6, 58; for human resource development education, 61–62; initiation of, 60–62; institutionalist forces and, 63–64; overview, 53–55; process, 56–59; self-study and, 58

Accreditation, certification, and credentialing (ACC), 103–111; competency frameworks, 105; definitions of, 57–58; in evaluation, 104–108; historical themes and implications for, 12–13; impact of diversification on, 15–17; modern evaluation related to, 8–10; outside of evaluation, 108–110; overview, 103–104

AEA. *See* American Evaluation Association (AEA)

Alkin, M. C., 8, 62, 65

Allegrante, J. P., 108

Altschuld, J. W., 3, 5, 6, 9, 11, 19, 40, 42, 43, 49, 53, 55, 56, 88, 89, 103, 106–108

Ambrosini, V., 63

American Evaluation Association (AEA), 5, 7, 15, 55

American Psychological Association (APA), 99

Andrews, B. K., 54, 55, 59, 60

Apostolou, B., 55

Association to Advance Collegiate Schools of Business (AACSB), 59–61

Auld, M. E., 108

Austin, W. W., 55, 59, 63

Azzam T., 49

B

Babidge, W. J., 109

Baron, M., 88, 89

Barry, M. M., 108

Barton, H., 63

Beehler, J. M., 54, 56, 59, 65

Benson, D., 54, 55, 63–65

Bentrem, D. J., 109

Bertrand, W., 24

Bickman, L., 55, 88

Bilder, A. E., 43

Bilimoria, K., 109

Billsberry, J., 63

Bober, M. J., 24–27, 41

Boisvert, Y., 53

Borys, S., 72, 73, 75, 77, 78, 82

Botje, D., 109

Boulet, J., 109

Bovee, S. L., 54, 55, 59, 60

Buchanan, H., 72, 75, 83, 84

Buscemi, D., 109

Bustello, M., 103

C

Canadian Evaluation Practice, 73–77

Canadian Evaluation Society (CES), 71–84; competencies for Canadian Evaluation Practice, 75–77; Credentialing Board, 80; foundations for profession, 72–73; practice-based membership of, 72

Canadian Journal of Program Evaluation, 15, 28

Caruthers, F. A., 29, 30

Certification/Credentialing, 6, 57, 87–101; in Canada, 17; criteria for judgement, 96–97; definition of, 6, 57; evaluation survey on, 89–98; governance of, 98; overview, 87–89

CES. *See* Canadian Evaluation Society (CES)

Chartered Institute of Personnel and Development (CIPD), 62

Chelimsky, E., 61

Chen, H., 40

Chen, J., 109

Cho, Y., 55, 61, 62

Christie, C. A., 39, 40

Chung, J. W., 109

CIPD. *See* Chartered Institute of Personnel and Development (CIPD)

Clark, T. R., 110

Clay, T., 40, 42, 43

Cohen, D. J., 62

Collins, P. M., 50

Competence, definition of, 23

Competencies, evaluator, 21–34; applications of, 28–29; for Canadian Evaluation Practice, 75–77; current status of, 24–30; definition of, 23–24; development and validation of, 33; effect and effectiveness of, 34; implications of, 30–32; overview, 21–23; program evaluation and, 32–34; taxonomies, 26–27; teaching evaluation with, 33–34; updates, 29–30

Competencies-based professional designations program, 77–79

Conner, R. F., 25, 40, 42, 43

Conrad, C. F., 43

Core Body of Knowledge (CBK) study, 73

Coryn, C. L. S., 23

Cousins, J., 74

Cousins, J. B., 53, 54, 61, 64, 83

ORDER FORM SUBSCRIPTION AND SINGLE ISSUES

DISCOUNTED BACK ISSUES:

Use this form to receive 20% off all back issues of *New Directions for Evaluation*.
All single issues priced at **$23.20** (normally $29.00)

TITLE	ISSUE NO.	ISBN

Call 1-800-835-6770 or see mailing instructions below. When calling, mention the promotional code JBNND to receive your discount. For a complete list of issues, please visit www.josseybass.com/go/ev

SUBSCRIPTIONS: (1 YEAR, 4 ISSUES)

☐ New Order   ☐ Renewal

U.S.	☐ Individual: $89	☐ Institutional: $358
CANADA/MEXICO	☐ Individual: $89	☐ Institutional: $398
ALL OTHERS	☐ Individual: $113	☐ Institutional: $432

Call 1-800-835-6770 or see mailing and pricing instructions below.
Online subscriptions are available at www.onlinelibrary.wiley.com

ORDER TOTALS:

Issue / Subscription Amount: $ _____

Shipping Amount: $ _____
(for single issues only – subscription prices include shipping)

Total Amount: $ _____

SHIPPING CHARGES:	
First Item	$6.00
Each Add'l Item	$2.00

(No sales tax for U.S. subscriptions. Canadian residents, add GST for subscription orders. Individual rate subscriptions must be paid by personal check or credit card. Individual rate subscriptions may not be resold as library copies.)

BILLING & SHIPPING INFORMATION:

☐ **PAYMENT ENCLOSED:** *(U.S. check or money order only. All payments must be in U.S. dollars.)*

☐ **CREDIT CARD:**   ☐ VISA   ☐ MC   ☐ AMEX

Card number _____Exp. Date_____

Card Holder Name_____Card Issue # _____

Signature _____Day Phone_____

☐ **BILL ME:** *(U.S. institutional orders only. Purchase order required.)*

Purchase order # _____
Federal Tax ID 13559302 • GST 89102-8052

Name_____

Address_____

Phone_____ E-mail_____

Copy or detach page and send to: **John Wiley & Sons, One Montgomery Street, Suite 1000,
San Francisco, CA 94104-4594**

Order Form can also be faxed to: **888-481-2665**

PROMO JBNND